Flannery O'Connor:
the Woman, the Thinker, the Visionary

¤

Books by Ted R. Spivey

*Flannery O'Connor: The Woman, the Thinker,
the Visionary* (1995)

Conrad Aiken: A Priest of Consciousness (1990)
(with Arthur Waterman)

Beyond Modernism: Toward a New Myth Criticism (1988)

Revival: Southern Writers in the Modern City (1986)

*The Writer as Shaman: The Pilgrimages of Conrad Aiken
and Walker Percy* (1986)

The Journey beyond Tragedy (1980)

The Coming of the New Man (1970)

¤

Flannery O'Connor:
the Woman, the Thinker, the Visionary

Ted R. Spivey

Mercer University Press
6316 Peake Road
Macon, Georgia 31210-3960

ISBN 0-86554-467-0

Flannery O'Connor:
The Woman, the Thinker, the Visionary
by Ted R. Spivey

Copyright © 1995
Mercer University Press, Macon, Georgia 31210-3960 USA

Library of Congress Cataloging-in-Publication Data

Spivey, Ted Ray, 1927–
    Flannery O'Connor: the woman, the thinker, the visionary/ Ted
R. Spivey.
    179 + viii pp.   6x9"
    Includes index.
    ISBN 0-86554-467-0
    1. O'Connor, Flannery—Criticism and interpretation. 2. Women
and literature—Southern States—History—20th century. 3. Women
—Southern States—Intellectual life.   4. Southern States—In
literature. 5. Prophecies in Literature.   I. Title.
PS3565.C57Z865   1994
813'.54—dc20   94-42344
                                                    CIP

Contents

Abbreviations

The abbreviations of O'Connor's works commonly cited in the text refer to the following editions:

CS   *The Complete Stories*. Introduced by Robert Giroux. New York: Farrar, Straus, and Giroux, 1986.

ERMC   *Everything That Rises Must Converge*. Introduced by Robert Fitzgerald. New York: Farrar, Straus, and Giroux, 1965.

HB   *The Habit of Being: Letters of Flannery O'Connor*. Edited by Sally Fitzgerald. New York: Farrar, Straus, and Giroux, 1979.

MM   *Mystery and Manners: Occasional Prose*. Edited by Sally and Robert Fitzgerald. New York: Farrar, Straus, and Giroux, 1969.

VBIA   *The Violent Bear It Away*. New York: Farrar, Straus, and Cudahy, 1960.

WB   *Wise Blood*. New York: Noonday Press, 1962.

¤

The publication of this volume is made possible by a generous grant from the John and Mary Franklin Foundation, Atlanta, Georgia.

¤

¤

for Mary Leta

¤

Introduction

Flannery O'Connor has become established in the canon of modern Southern writers as a figure second only to William Faulkner. Sometime during the 1980s, in the estimation of most critics, she passed Eudora Welty in that list of women who in letters had plumbed the depths of Southern life and Southern culture. As brilliant as the stories and novels of Welty are, they lack for many careful readers a full probing of the roots of both Southern violence and Southern emotionalism, especially as expressed in the varied religious responses of the region.

More than Welty and more than any other Southern writer except Faulkner, O'Connor plumbed the depths of race, religion, family, and class structure in the South. And, in a way that Faulkner and no other Southern writer has done, she presented in her best stories and in her two novels visions of both the collapse of a Southern agrarian life that existed during the better part of four centuries and the possibility of the renewal of life in the Southern United States in terms of new megalopolises like Atlanta. This claim for O'Connor may at first seem to be far too great for a writer who published as little as she did and who, as so many of her critics have suggested, wrote about a narrow range of subjects. But within that narrow range and within her brief pages, she communicated far more than most modern writers in books of much greater length.

Along with the critical acclaim that O'Connor had begun to receive, late in her career came a slowly developing cult that was so small at first that she was not even aware of it. But this cult has continued to grow since her death, so much so that in 1988 the Associated Press noted that "A mysterious pull compels some readers of Milledgeville author Flannery O'Connor to become obsessed with her." The report states that her cult followers "want to read everything she has written and learn all they can about her. They want to see where she lived and wrote, where she attended school, where she is buried." It also notes the growing number of those who "make their pilgrimage to Milledgeville to pay homage" and the continuing fact that "Local residents often are not aware of the interest their city has for the author's devotees" and that "there is little public recognition of Miss O'Connor" in her hometown.[1]

---

[1]*The Atlanta Journal and Constitution*, 20 March 1988, B7.

The only other Georgia writer who regularly draws devotees to her hometown and to her grave site is Atlanta's Margaret Mitchell, author of *Gone with the Wind*, a book O'Connor had little use for. In fact, from the beginning of her career, O'Connor saw herself to be what literary critics usually call a "serious writer," one who sought not commercial success but rather a place among those individuals who would achieve some kind of distinction in the literature of her country, small though it might be (she thought, incorrectly, her fame would at best be small). For O'Connor, Margaret Mitchell, a literary heroine of enormous dimensions to the average Georgia reader, was "a commercial writer." It was probably Margaret Mitchell more than anyone else that she was referring to in a 1953 letter to Sally and Robert Fitzgerald: "My kinfolks think I am a commercial writer now and really they are proud of me. My uncle Louis [Cline] is always bringing me a message from somebody at The King Hardware, Co. who has read *Wise Blood*. The last was: ask her why she don't write about some nice people. Louis says, I told them you wrote what *paid*" (*HB*, 54).

O'Connor lived with full acceptance of and with generally a good-humored attitude toward the commercialized literary views of her family, including those of her mother and of most of the people of Milledgeville. And she firmly insisted when I first met her in 1958 and at other times when I talked with her that she was in no way a writer "alienated" (her term always when bringing up the subject) from the community in which she lived. The meaning of the term "alienated" and the concepts surrounding it I will return to later, because her non-alienation on one level and her alienation on another one, I believe, are central to understanding both her life and her work. No writer on her work has dealt at any length with the complicated interplay between these two conditions of her life in the South.

In one of her several literary roles, O'Connor was, like Margaret Mitchell, a woman speaking to her fellow Southerners of all classes and types about what was for them a very serious matter. It was the matter of social cataclysm, and the two women spoke not as intellectuals but as writers of fictional presentations of this social cataclysm. That cataclysm for both was the suffering caused in the South by the Great Depression of the thirties and the earlier, profounder cataclysm of the near collapse after the Civil War of Southern culture itself. As Southerners, both women carried within themselves conscious and unconscious minds that struggled with collective memories of group suffering. As women, they faced the decline and even collapse of family values, the exposure of children, and the failure of men in leadership roles to solve basic economic and social problems, a failure that made it necessary for women both in the Reconstruction era and in the thirties to play a role not then usually allotted to them.

Unlike Mitchell, who wrote about the nineteenth century, O'Connor set her work in the forties and early fifties of this century, a time when the South had experienced an upswing in confidence due to the prosperity that accompanied World War II, but many of the painful scenes of both physical and psychic poverty found, for instance, in *Wise Blood*, doubtless sprang from O'Connor's own memories of the depressed thirties, especially the scenes involving dispossessed children and young people. For the South especially, the Great Depression did not end until America was actually engaged in hostilities. And the late forties, the period after the war, in turn presented the region with social and economic problems which included a national downswing in the economy, the probability of a Republican victory in 1948 with the recurring prospect of a tight money economy that Southerners had since Reconstruction feared in Republican administrations. And, possibly most painful of all, was the growing liberalization of the Democratic party in the Truman administration, a fearful prospect for conservatives that led in 1948 to the creation of a totally ineffective Dixiecrat Party, which impossibly sought to give the South its own political voice.

With the South caught between an industrial-based Republicanism and a Northern liberal-controlled Democratic party, fear grew concerning a new, returning poverty and the possibility of the overthrow of long-entrenched Jim Crow laws. Since Reconstruction, the South had associated the decline and possible death of its culture with poverty and with black political domination. The Democratic party had meant from Grover Cleveland to Franklin D. Roosevelt a chance to rise from destitution to some measure of economic and cultural self-determination without a corresponding disturbance of white supremacy. The South's political agony in the late forties is not recorded directly in O'Connor's published work of the early fifties, but there is recorded in *Wise Blood* and *A Good Man Is Hard to Find* a woman's awareness of neglected children, of broken families, of racial unrest, of bitter prejudice against blacks and "foreigners" who might take jobs from white Southerners, of confidence men hoodwinking innocents, men reminiscent of earlier carpetbaggers and scalawags depicted in *Gone with the Wind*. In her fiction, O'Connor often looked through the eyes of prejudiced Southerners, but at other times her own irony concerning Southern self-deceptions shines through, along with her pity for a culture continually reminded of past suffering due to both economic and human failure.

O'Connor majored in social science at the Georgia State College for Women in her hometown of Milledgeville, and her now well-known remark about being saved from social science by the grace of God is often quoted by those who emphasize the religious side of O'Connor. Yet her penetrating vision of many aspects of Southern society in the first half of the twentieth century must never be lost sight of in a concern for her religious vision, as it has been by many of her best critics of the past twenty years. Lewis P. Simpson, an extremely perceptive critic of Southern letters and history, probably emphasizes too much the seeming divorce between O'Connor's religious and her historical visions:

> She lacks, perhaps refuses, an intimacy with history. Blessed by an overpowering gift of faith, she lets the Faulkner company, the survivors of history, go its way. Her vision is directed toward timeless order and the ultimate beatitude of the soul. Prophesying the irresistibility of God's grace in the life of the individual, her stories follow a compelling aesthetic of revelation. The result is that, in spite of their detailed portrayal of the manners of her region, they divest it of a tension toward historical reality.[2]

The agony of historical suffering shines through the best fiction of O'Connor, much as it does through that of Eudora Welty, whose early work O'Connor greatly admired. Both Welty and O'Connor have that "detailed portrayal of manners" of the South, to use Simpson's term, that modern readers often expect to find, but both women also indirectly and even at times directly attack with wit and irony the failure of Southern leaders—often men but, especially in O'Connor's work, sometimes powerful women—to address the problems of Southern society as a whole.

Thus, in O'Connor's fiction, those most experiencing the brunt of Southern poverty and its accompanying problems—blacks and poor whites—are forced to seek solutions to social and economic problems in worn-out religious formulas. Only in a few stories, most notably "The

---

[2]Lewis P. Simpson, *The Brazen Face of History* (Baton Rouge: Louisiana State University Press, 1980) 248.

Artificial Nigger" and "Revelation," does O'Connor effectively reveal what Simpson calls the irresistibility of God's grace. Even though she reveals sympathy for her culturally deprived religious questers, she makes no bones about the general failure of their religious frenzy. With minds haunted by Christ, they generally do violence either to themselves or to others. Without knowing it, their religious frenzy and its violent manifestations are directed not so much against sin—the widely proclaimed enemy—but against a rigid hierarchy of money and power that deals with them and their black antagonists as it has dealt with them since the seventeenth century: as minor cogs in a great plantation, an agribusiness machine that, like the American-Spanish empire it was in part modeled on, continually requires victims.

As I hope to suggest in the chapters that follow, Flannery O'Connor viewed Southern society as both a member at the top of the hierarchy and as one who, though not always fully aware of it, was, with her mordant irony, on the side of the ignorant, dispossessed farmers and their oppressed wives and their often neglected children. As one who grew up in two of the most rigidly hierarchical urban areas of Georgia, Savannah and Milledgeville, both having been for a time capitals of Georgia during the brightest days of Southern cultural self-confidence, O'Connor was fully aware of the nuances of life around her. When she said of herself, as she often did to friends, that she was not an alienated writer in the town of Milledgeville, she meant that she was an accepted member of the town's dominant minority, which she was. Yet, as a writer who was self-consciously "serious" and not "commercial," she was alienated inevitably from many people of all classes in the South. Her fiction, of course, is filled with children with intellectual pretensions who are continually at war with old-fashioned hierarchical parents, particularly plantation-remembering mothers. Yet O'Connor's fiction also shows as deep a sympathy for the bewildered mother as it does for the recalcitrant child, and often more sympathy. This ability to have it both ways—to be on the side of the hierarchical rulers and at the same time on the side of those suffering under them—lends a complexity to O'Connor's work found in few recent Southern titles.

In many ways O'Connor resembled Ellen Glasgow, who with what she called "blood and irony," first began to write a truly modernist Southern fiction. Yet Glasgow, while capturing brilliantly the hierarchies of Richmond in her Queenborough novels, never dug deeply into the life of the dispossessed whites who envy, admire, and despise a ruling class that, for several centuries, had pitted them against their black dependents and had snickered at their outlandish religion and their continuing poverty. Nor does Glasgow's fiction capture the agonies of blacks in the South. What Glasgow missed, above all else, in her portrayal of postbellum Southern life was the false rigidity of the hierarchy in its dealings with both white and black underclasses. Only a woman like O'Connor, who was both of the hierarchy and not of it—one with a full awareness of the complexity both of the hierarchy and of its failure to properly care for those on the lower rungs of the social scale—could possibly have written a fiction that was at once brilliant in social details but also profound in its philosophical and religious viewpoints.

O'Connor then was socially and religiously both an insider and an outsider. As a religious and philosophical outsider she often has been studied, but, as a social insider who accepted (and understood more than did most writers) her historical milieu, O'Connor has not been very well understood. Nor, I think, has her particular connection with the women's movement, both in her own lifetime and since, been properly assessed. Her relationship to the role of women in historical Southern culture can now be more clearly seen with the increasing awareness of woman's historical part in the culture of the South.

Elizabeth Fox-Genovese's work in the area of Southern women and slavery, particularly her book *Within the Plantation Household: Black and White Women in the Old South*, reveals the power of the Southern white woman in the hierarchy.[3] Her work is, as one article suggests, an attack on the " 'New Englandization' of the history of Southern women," which has depicted them as "mainly housewives struggling against the outsized domestic responsibilities of their plantation," and discusses Southern women as "proto-feminists and even abolitionists."[4] Fox-Genovese has written about women of slaveholding families, those families from which grew the distinctive Southern ruling class that held firmly to its position in the cities and towns which O'Connor knew best. These women played a key role in maintaining a kind of rigid class system that

---

[3]Elizabeth Fox-Genovese, *Within the Plantation Household: Black and White Women of the Old South* (Chapel Hill: University of North Carolina Press, 1988). This book, among other things, establishes certain ways in which Southern culture differs from Northern culture and sees these differences in terms of the evolving rule of Southern hierarchical women.

[4]Roy Pattishall, "Plantation Voices," *Emory Magazine* 63/5 (January 1988): 20.

used and abused most blacks and the many white people contemptuously referred to by the white ruling class and its black house servants as "white trash," the very people O'Connor often found, for fictional purposes, the most interesting people in the South to write about, particularly in terms of religious belief.

The hierarchy's lofty attitude toward the poor, Fox-Genovese believes, grew directly from the actions of powerful women even more than from those of influential men, especially after the Civil War when men suffered from a loss of self-esteem due to defeat. Thus Fox-Genovese explained: "I'm arguing that . . . the women contributed more powerfully than the men to the hierarchical distancing between classes in Southern society."[5] In *Within the Plantation Household*, Fox-Genovese revealed how slavery was an everyday part of the privileged Southern woman's environment, and from this acute awareness of her relationship with blacks grew that woman's belief in her superiority to all black women and to white women outside the ruling class. As a member of the white ruling class in the rural and small-town South, O'Connor understood well the matriarchal Southern women of the first half of this century, in that period before desegregation and the triumph of the civil rights movement. But O'Connor was also an "outsider" in the ruling white class structure like those of her characters both male and female who continually challenge in her fiction a Southern matriarch who has one foot planted in the past and the other in the present.

So much has been written about the religious views of O'Connor that the large body of official and sometimes rather worshipful scholarship and criticism that has grown up around her work has largely ignored O'Connor the secular intellectual. This side of the author opposed the rigid Southern social system that was not seriously shaken until the civil rights revolution of the sixties. Robert Coles, possibly more than anyone else, has grasped the meaning of both the secular intellectual and secular modern artist within O'Connor's makeup, as well as her own struggle with many aspects of secular intellectualism within herself and her many friends. Thus Coles can write that "It is necessary to take seriously what came to be an 'affair' of sorts; Flannery O'Connor and her passionately insistent involvement with people of her own (intellectual) kind, if not,

---

[5]Ibid.

commonly, her own faith."[6] O'Connor saw the many social failures of the ruling hierarchy of men and women, and, while at times defending the hierarchy, she believed, like most American secular intellectuals, that at least some of these failures could and should be set right. Where she disagreed with secular intellectuals, as Coles pointed out, was in their utopianism. Thus Coles wrote: "The secular messianic mentality was not hers; she mocked it—a critically important element in her writing. But she wasn't sitting on a plantation with a gun, daring some federal marshals to come get her."[7] Coles suggested that O'Connor "had no great love for social science" because of "the prideful excess of generalization to be found in some of the sociological and psychological journals"—journals of the sort she read as a social science major in college.[8]

As a social scientist and psychologist, Coles himself does not deny the importance of O'Connor as a social critic. In fact, he sees in her work a love of the sociological "concrete, the particular" similar to the kind of sociology practiced by David Riesman, whose "career as a sociologist, essayist, observer of his fellow citizens, has been characterized by a remarkably brilliant and faithful dedication to the specifics of American life."[9] In the name of both the specifics of social life and of a vision anchored in her inherited Roman Catholic tradition, O'Connor viewed a South which was, as she began to write about it, beginning to undergo a profounder metamorphosis than any it had known as a region since the Civil War and Reconstruction, one the region is still involved in and one that may well bring an end to Southern culture as we have known it—although there is, in the nineties, a continuing reaffirmation of many aspects of this particular regional culture.

O'Connor's role as social critic was linked with her awareness of herself as both a serious writer and as a religious philosopher of sorts. When she began to see herself in the late forties as a full-time "serious" writer, it may be argued that she found in the South only one role model, Eudora Welty, whose reputation was then not nearly what it is today. Like Carson McCullers, a writer she never felt any affinity for, O'Connor, after studying creative writing in Iowa, went to New York to seek

---

[6]Robert Coles, *Flannery O'Connor's South* (Baton Rouge: Louisiana State University Press, 1980) xxvi.
[7]Ibid.
[8]Ibid, xxviii.
[9]Ibid.

a place for herself as a serious writer. But the first appearance of lupus—the disease she suffered, often painfully, the rest of her life—soon made it impossible to live anywhere but with her mother on her dairy farm near Milledgeville. But on that farm another "serious" Southern writer not very well known outside academic circles—Caroline Gordon—found her and provided her with a kind of literary mentor that American women seldom, if ever, knew in the past. O'Connor also had what amounted to a literary-artistic sister relationship with the anonymous correspondent "A," whose letters evoked some of O'Connor's deepest remarks about the life of the mind and the work of the literary artist.

Caroline Gordon helped O'Connor to work out a religious philosophy that was basically conservative and anti-utopian in nature, one resembling certain views held by Agrarians like Allen Tate, Gordon's husband of many years. Yet, as I will later suggest, this philosophy is only one aspect of a larger religious philosophy that she believed in, one that grew directly out of her reading of Catholic theologians. Marion Montgomery's book *Why Flannery O'Connor Stayed at Home* is the longest and most scholarly statement yet made about this consciously developed philosophy. Its relationship to O'Connor's feminism will be considered in chapters that follow. Critics like Montgomery who have studied O'Connor's thought would probably argue that O'Connor was in no way a feminist. As anyone who has read her letters knows, she was too outwardly conventional, too conservative, too much the old-fashioned Catholic to be similar to most contemporary feminists. Yet she was, I believe, far more of a feminist than she herself knew. What we now call the contemporary American feminist movement dates largely from the early sixties with Betty Friedan's *The Feminine Mystique* serving as a kind of watershed in the women's movement in America. O'Connor would have been far too "messianic" for Friedan, but what writer of fiction deals so well as O'Connor with the collapse of the feminine mystique as we see that mystique embodied in certain Southern women of the mid-century?

O'Connor in her work also revealed her understanding of two other feminist issues that have engaged younger feminists in the quarter century since Betty Friedan's first book. These are the continuing problems of care for children while mothers and fathers are both working and of the need to achieve balanced relationships between men and women, a problem that for O'Connor was often seen in mid-century Southern terms of strong women and weak, confused men. O'Connor, as a writer who was often but not always sociological, presented her fictional vision of these problems that have occupied many feminists in both fiction and nonfiction, but, like many of her sisters, she had no easy answers to individual and social problems. As a religious thinker, she recommended faith and love, but in her fiction we find little of either, though the kinds of problems women are beset with in this century abound in her fiction.

The need to explore the role of woman as both intellectual and writer was one of the reasons I first sought a meeting with Flannery O'Connor. I had completed in 1954 a doctoral dissertation comparing the work of Thomas Hardy and George Eliot. I had for some years been reading women writers, searching in the contemporary literature of America for someone like George Eliot or Virginia Woolf who combined a powerful intellect with marked gifts for writing fiction. Finally, in 1957, I began to read O'Connor's fiction, and the next year I worked up enough courage to write her and ask if I could talk with her about her writing and her connections with other writers like herself. She responded affirmatively, and I began a correspondence and a series of visits to her home, which was only a hundred miles from Atlanta where I taught at Georgia State University. Our conversations and letters turned into serious literary, philosophical, psychological, and theological discussions. I came to her with a marked interest in the modern woman as writer and found a thinker, a social and literary critic, and a multifaceted novelist.

I have already mentioned the outsider-insider aspects of O'Connor's makeup, which I would only gradually discover as I came to know her better. There was another, even more important tension in her nature—the tension between her conservative Catholic vision, similar in many ways to Allen Tate's, and her modernist, sociologically trained intellect. Robert Fitzgerald has called our attention to how much she resembles T. S. Eliot. William Empson once told Stephen Spender that Eliot had a medieval mind, and the same, I think, can be said for O'Connor. What I believe is deepest in her writing is a tension that exists between her medieval self and her modernist self.

From our arguments with others we make rhetoric, Yeats said, but from our arguments with ourself we make poetry. The struggle within her, partly conscious and partly unconscious, accounts for the strangely visionary quality of O'Connor's fiction. The essential poetry in her best writing is contained within what I call the O'Connor vision. But to approach this vision, I think it is first necessary to come fully to grips with

O'Connor the woman both as writer and as Southerner, and this I attempt to do in the first section, "The Woman." In the second section, "The Thinker," I seek to relate her critical, modernist intellect with her development as a writer who was partly, but by no means totally, connected with the Southern literary renascence through her chief mentor Caroline Gordon and Gordon's husband Allen Tate. In this section I seek to examine O'Connor as both a literary and social critic and as an emerging woman of letters, whose significance, had she lived, might have had a even more profound influence on the development of contemporary Southern writing. Finally, in the third section, "The Visionary," I will relate the woman and the thinker to what still seems to many of her readers a strange and at times tangled vision based on a kind of modern Protestant prophecy and a Catholic awareness of sacrament. I should also note for the reader that my study of O'Connor is more of a remembrance in the first section, more of an analytical study in the final two, and, of course, more personal again in the epilogue. I believe that my choice of this format is best justified by the nature of the sections themselves, and I hope that the reader shares my opinion. While she was Flannery to me after I first made her acquaintance, I adopt in this study the formal convention of referring to my friend by her full name or her surname O'Connor.

For all her poetic and visionary intensity, I believe Flannery O'Connor to be a woman and writer very much rooted in the history of mid-century America. In spite of the difficulty of her work, she still speaks to personal and social issues of the last decades of this century because much of what she found to be troubling in the period of the late forties, fifties, and early sixties is now of greater concern to most people than it was in her own time.

I.
The Woman

Chapter 1

The Woman as Anima

Sitting on the porch of the white, two-story farmhouse at Andalusia for the first time in that late summer of 1958, I studied carefully the woman that I had already come to believe, largely on the basis of my own literary intuition, was the most significant Southern writer of her time. I had read only one volume of her stories, *A Good Man Is Hard to Find*, and, in fact, had found several of these stories to be of little consequence. The good ones, however, had imaginative power, I believed then and believe now, greater than any I had seen in a writer of my own generation. Flannery O'Connor was only two years older than I was, and she was from the same part of Georgia in which I grew up. We had age and place in common, and that is a lot for two people to begin with who happen to be from the South. When she found out, after brief opening remarks, that I had taken a course under Allen Tate at the University of Minnesota in 1953, she seemed to find herself conversationally where she wanted to be, which was talking about writing and writers.

I had come to O'Connor knowing little about her except her stories and the fact that she lived on a farm near Milledgeville, a town I always passed through whenever I went from Atlanta, where I taught English in an urban college, to visit my parents in Swainsboro. I had never met anyone who knew her, and I had little knowledge of her literary and intellectual antecedents. In my letter asking to visit her, I stated my interest in the religious aspect of her work and asked if, as a Catholic novelist, she had been influenced by Graham Greene or Evelyn Waugh. In her brief reply she said that her chief influences as a Catholic novelist were the French novelists Georges Bernanos and François Mauriac. She also said that she wrote in the mornings but was free in the afternoons and that I should appear at 2:00 P.M. on the date I had asked for, which I did on my August visit to my parents. When I knocked on her door, she appeared in a light-colored, rather conservative dress and suggested that we sit in rocking chairs on her porch. She asked me a few questions about myself, and within five minutes we were talking about writers and about their connection, when they had any, with religion. The talk lasted about two hours and was intense.

Sally Fitzgerald, the editor of the O'Connor letters, introduced my correspondence with O'Connor by stating that I am the "author of two books on literature and myth." Fitzgerald then wrote that "he had called to pay his respects" and that "a long correspondence began with this letter" *(HB,* 294). My scholarly interest then and now, amounting some-times to a passion, is in fact the study of myth and modern literature, a subject that for me includes a consideration of connections between religion and modern literature.

I did pay my respects to Miss O'Connor that summer of 1958, but mainly I came to talk to her, quite directly, about her work and the subject of religion and literature. I found then and later that, though she would never have much to say about her own work, she would have a great deal to say about writers and their mythic and religious viewpoints. She had a way of getting right to the point, and yet she was often oblique in her conversations, bringing in during those two first hours I spent with her a large amount of literary gossip, some sharply presented, which I responded to in kind, quite happily. I left her that day feeling wrung out after both an intense intellectual exchange and an afternoon of gossip and assessment of contemporary writers, most of whom were put down rather firmly by the quite serious author. I left wondering what kind of impression I had made on her. I wondered even if she liked me at all because I could sense certain deep and sometimes disturbing currents running through her. Much later I would learn that, in all of her complexity (and she was the most complex person I have ever met), she could, with various other people, make entirely different types of conversation, all of which seemed quite sincere to those who knew her.

Even before I had the chance to write her a note of thanks for allowing me to come to see her, I received at the home of my parents in Swainsboro a letter that began "I have just finished a book which I am sure you would find relevant to your train of thought. This is *Israel and Revelation* by Eric Voegelin . . . It has to do with history as being existence under God, the 'leap in being,' etc" *(HB,* 294). She had sized up my train of thought exactly and had directed me to a writer I knew only by reputation and one that I would read very soon with profit, even borrowing her copy of the book. The last sentence of the letter pleased me even more: "I enjoyed your visit and hope you will stop in again if you find it convenient when you pass this way" *(HB,* 295).

After our first meeting, I saw her several times a year until the final time in 1962. We corresponded until early 1964, when the growing illness made it hard for her to write. For all the depth of her letters, it was the conversations that most moved me because very soon we were more than two people talking about subjects such as literature and religion. We were friends who both had serious doubts concerning religion itself as a force in the world, one that had largely been put aside by modern humanity. And, finally, she had grave doubts about my own beliefs, often confused as they were, and she expressed those doubts about my beliefs to me in conversation as well as in letters to me and to others. Yet, in spite of everything, we remained friends, even though her last letter to me, of 17 March 1964, is in places harsh. She had, as letters to some of her best friends show, a way of very plain speaking about ideas and personal matters, but her way of speaking did not, even when there was anger, cause her to be any less a friend.

The directness of O'Connor's response to actions or ideas that she disapproved of was almost the opposite of what anyone in the fifties would have expected of a "Southern lady," a role she could play as well as anyone I know, because she was very deeply a lady in every sense of that word. But the closer the friend, sometimes the more devastating the assault, as in the case of her reply to Robert Lowell when he announced he was leaving the Church. Lowell was not only a close friend and a literary companion that she first met in 1949 at Yaddo, the writer's colony in upstate New York, but he was a man she might have been in love with if circumstances had been different. The essence of her attack on Lowell seems to have been summed up in a letter of 26 April 1954 to Sally and Robert Fitzgerald: "I wrote him that his not being in the Church was a grief to me and I knew no more to say about it. I said I severely doubted he would do any good to anybody else outside but that it was probably true he would do good to himself inasmuch as he would be the only one in a position to" (*HB*, 71). Here we see the side of O'Connor's mind anchored in traditional Catholicism. She said, in effect, that Lowell could do no good to anyone outside the Church and that, separate from the Church, no one could do anything good for him. Her anger toward "A" for leaving the Church was just as sharp, and the anger she directed at me often had to do with my own attitudes toward the Church. Her despair with my attitudes toward Catholicism reached a low point in 1960, as we see it recorded in a letter to "A" in which she lamented that she did not know enough about the Church to properly instruct me. This attitude of hers was so significant in our relationship that I will return to it later in this section because it had an important bearing on our differing attitudes toward the role of the feminine in art and history.

O'Connor was, even early in her career, reported by some who met her to have a difficult and sometimes painful personality. As her stature as a writer grew, even in her own lifetime, she was sometimes pictured by those who had met her as a woman who made profound statements about literature and life and, by some, as a woman of an almost saintly nature who bore her many burdens, physical and otherwise, with patience and humility. Both the saint and the woman of wise statements were present in her makeup, but, like any complex person, she was many people. She was aware of the bad impression she sometimes made on others, and there was at least one good reason why this should be so, a reason which she clearly stated to "A" in a 16 November 1957 letter:

> Your visit was thoroughly enjoyed by us and is always good for me though I may look tired. The truth is I am tired every afternoon and there's nothing to be done about it. It's the nature of the disease. A lot of people decide I am bored or indifferent or uppity but at a certain hour of the day my motor cuts off automatically (*HB*, 252).

O'Connor's disease, lupus, was not the only reason for the tiredness she confessed to. She wrote every morning, six days a week, and she wrote with a profound concentration. Rightly, she said that she wrote every morning and spent the rest of the day recovering. It was in the period of recovering, the afternoons, that she generally talked with visitors. All of my conversations with her began about two o'clock.

I must say immediately that at no time in our conversations did she ever appear tired, bored, or indifferent, though others have said she sometimes did appear tired. She often spoke to me and others as a New Englander traditionally did in conversation rather than as a Southerner. Southerners like Thomas Jefferson never disagreed in conversation with anyone out of politeness; John Adams, on the other hand, spoke his mind and said what he wanted to, even if it might lead to disagreement. I liked O'Connor for speaking directly and getting her emotions involved in the conversation. Her anger toward me, which appeared occasionally in both letters and conversations because of a statement I might make about the Church or some other subject, generally pleased me.

My relationship with O'Connor was similar to that of two women of her own generation, Louise Abbot and the anonymous correspondent "A," as well as to that of William A. Sessions, a college professor of our generation who often visited her and was a regular correspondent. Sally Fitzgerald recorded that when "A" first wrote in 1955, O'Connor "was obviously hungry for conversation on matters of primary interest to her, and she found with her new correspondent exactly the kind of exchange she needed" (*HB*, 89). In Louise Abbot, O'Connor found a correspondent who was not only a published writer and a graduate of the University of North Carolina, but one who shared her intense concern with problems of religion. Also, in Abbot, she found a correspondent who, living only fifty miles away, came from a Georgia town very similar to Milledgeville, the town of Louisville, which had been the Georgia capital before Milledgeville. Insight into the problem of the woman in the South who is also a writer and an intellectual can be found in letters to Abbot as well as in Abbot's extremely insightful memoir of O'Connor that appeared in *The Southern Literary Journal* in 1970. O'Connor's friendship with Sessions, also a graduate of the University of North Carolina and later a Ph.D. in English from Columbia University, grew in part out of his being a fellow Catholic, a writer, and a scholar-critic. Sessions was, when he first met O'Connor, an English professor at West Georgia College and in 1966 became a member of the faculty of Georgia State University.

O'Connor's friendship with Ben Griffith, who taught English at nearby Bessie Tift Women's College in Forsyth, was heartening to her, and it provided her with yet another opportunity to discuss literature seriously with a college professor. She wrote Griffith on 9 July 1955 to thank him "for lending my books around to the scholars" and further stated: "I relish the idea of being read by scholars" (*HB*, 89). Unlike many American authors in this century, O'Connor was deeply respectful of literature teachers and had once herself considered becoming a teacher. As I found soon after I began my conversations with her, the Tates (Allen and Caroline Gordon), two of the greatest teachers of literature and creative writing to spring from the South in this century, were central to her thinking not only about her own writing but about literature in general. In the same letter to Griffith, she discussed Griffith's view and her own view of the protagonist Hazel Motes in *Wise Blood* and then added, "[I]n fact, Mrs. Tate wrote me that she thought the Bible salesman was a super Hazel Motes, one with all his evil potentialities" (*HB*, 89).

With William Sessions, she found not only a learned and subtle literary intelligence but also a Catholic convert intensely interested in the problems of religion. With "A" and Sessions, as well as with Abbot and myself, she found people who were concerned with both literature and religion. Robert and Sally Fitzgerald also played, along with other roles, this particular role in her life. The same had been true in her relationship with Robert Lowell earlier at Yaddo, but their friendship seemed to falter somewhat after he left the Church. With Sessions she had a friend, as her letters to him reveal, that she could talk to in detail about the Catholic Church, both locally and worldwide. With me she found one interested personally in liturgical religion, a Methodist moving toward the Anglican communion, following T. S. Eliot's example in many ways, but one who was never comfortable with the concept of ecclesiastical hierarchy, as Sessions clearly was. The struggles between us, both in her letters and in our conversations, were based in large part upon my inability to accept Catholic hierarchical thinking.

My own experience with O'Connor was in many ways like that of "A," who for a time was a Catholic and who eventually left the Church. In her first letter to "A," O'Connor congratulated her correspondent on recognizing "my work for what I try to make it." Then she defined her viewpoint quite clearly:

> I write the way I do because (not though) I am a Catholic. This is a fact and nothing covers it like the bald statement. However, I am a Catholic peculiarly possessed of the modern consciousness, that thing Jung describes as unhistorical, solitary, and guilty. To possess this *within* the Church is to bear a burden, the necessary burden for the conscious Catholic. It's to feel the contemporary situation at the ultimate level. I think the Church is the only thing that is going to make the terrible world we are coming to endurable (*HB*, 90).

I agree with O'Connor's assessments of herself as both Catholic and modernist and will in the chapters that follow continue to place her with other writers like herself—Caroline Gordon, of course, and also Eliot, Yeats, Bernanos, and Mauriac. But O'Connor was also a woman in America who ignored aspects of her modern feminine experience that even today places her, though Catholic, far more with some of her fellow women writers than it does with those Europeans like Mauriac and Bernanos that she said most inspired her. The one aspect of her view, however, that today few thinkers hold to, including most Catholic intellectuals, is that it is *only* the Church, in her words to "A," "that is going to make the terrible world we are coming to endurable." This concept smacked for non-Catholics of that period far too much of her strongly held belief that outside Catholicism there was little or no hope for salvation. O'Connor did not say in this letter that salvation comes from God, or Christ, but from a "thing," the "only thing" that will save the world from some coming barbarism. Yet later she could call the Protestant patriarch who is young Tarwater's uncle in *The Violent Bear It Away* a "natural" Catholic, and at various times she spoke to me as a Protestant in terms of what she called the "separated brothers." Still, she seemed to say that only the Church brings salvation because, as she put it in her first letter to "A," the Church "is somehow the body of Christ and that on this we are fed" (*HB*, 90).

Salvation, in the traditional sense of achieving eternal life, was, for O'Connor, obtained within the Church. She also believed that the Church alone could enable humanity to survive the new barbarism. For O'Connor, as for T. S. Eliot and W. B. Yeats, a new dark age was about to descend upon mankind. This was a view few Catholics held in America, where an optimism that sprang from the doctrine of progress was, in 1955, the dominant mood for nearly everyone. Thus, in the same 20 July 1955 letter to "A," she wrote that "It seems to be a fact that you have to suffer as much from the Church as for it" (*HB*, 90). Few, if any, Catholics she knew could understand the viewpoint of a dark age about to emerge and, if they could, would certainly have opposed her viewpoint. Yet she made it quite clear in the next paragraph of her first letter to "A" that she believed that for most people God is dead: "This is a generation of wingless chickens, which I suppose is what Nietzsche meant when he said God was dead" (*HB*, 90). After stating her anger at reviews which called her work "brutal and sarcastic," she then invoked the name of W. B. Yeats by paraphrasing the last lines of his poem "The Second Coming": "I believe that there are many rough beasts now slouching toward Bethlehem to be born and that I have reported the progress of a few of them, and when I see these stories described as horror stories I am always amused because the reviewer always has hold of the wrong horror" (*HB*, 90).

One of O'Connor's chief purposes in writing is described above—to warn of the coming of the rough beast, depicted in Yeats's "The Second Coming" as slouching toward Bethlehem to be born in a not-too-distant time. In the poem the modern age is described as one in which "darkness" has dropped once more. Thus, in this highly significant letter to a woman roughly her own age, one who would become, for a time, her profoundest intellectual companion, O'Connor cited three authorities who are in some of their best writing deeply apocalyptic: Jung, Nietzsche, and

Yeats. I believe that these three men formed the basis for a large part of her philosophical viewpoint as it related to the modern world. And I also believe that the modernist apocalyptic viewpoint that she absorbed from them and others like Max Picard, whose visionary book *The Flight from God* she urged me to read early in our friendship, found its way into her best writing. Her particular version of the modern apocalyptic viewpoint is surely one of the chief reasons why her work excites so much interest among the young. It was my own knowledge and acceptance of the kind of vision found in Yeats's "The Second Coming" that caused our conversations and letters to have, at certain times, an intensity they might not have otherwise had.

I make much of this first letter to "A" for several reasons. First, it shows how she could in one letter explain some of her basic views to a woman like herself and could also open herself very quickly to such a person, while at the same time avoiding the apocalyptic theme with most of her other correspondents. She obviously believed that few people were ready for the apocalyptic viewpoint. Yet she also had at least two other philosophical positions which I will discuss in a later chapter. Robert Coles, as I have earlier suggested, was aware of her doubts about what he calls most intellectuals. For O'Connor, most intellectuals were far too liberal and optimistic to be taken seriously. If the darkness of barbarism is now about to fall upon humanity, as she believed, then optimistic liberals could do little to help. Yet she had, as Coles has shown, a liberal sociological philosophy that she applied to what she considered to be that short period before barbarism would engulf everything. Also she held a view, gained largely from reading Eric Voegelin but also from knowing Allen Tate, Caroline Gordon, and John Crowe Ransom, that was best described by the younger Agrarian Cleanth Brooks as "modern gnosticism," the term that is also used by her contemporary Marion Montgomery, who has extensively analyzed this side of her thinking in his study *Why Flannery O'Connor Stayed at Home*. But I believe what she most deeply wanted to talk about, even more than about her largely traditional views of the Church, was modern apocalyptic thinking.

In October of 1958, O'Connor wrote to me these highly significant words: "I suppose what bothers us so much about writing about the return of modern people to a sense of the Holy Spirit is that the religious sense seems to be bred out of them in the kind of society we've lived in since the 18th century. And it's bred out of them double quick now by the religious substitute for religion" (*HB*, 299-300). There was at least

one unintentional irony in the letter, stated as follows: "All this is under-
lining the obvious but I am unaccustomed to finding anyone else interested in it" (*HB*, 300). What she believed about the modern apocalypse was
obvious to very few at that time, and, for that reason, she had found few
people she could easily talk to on this subject. I had been teaching Yeats
and Eliot for four years from an apocalyptic viewpoint and had found no
real interest in what I believed then and still do is the deepest theme in
their work. When I first met her, O'Connor believed that the modern
apocalypses she saw in progress should be obvious, but that very few
really could grasp its meaning. But today, if it is still not obvious to large
numbers, it at least is apprehended in part by millions; otherwise, Yeats's
poem "The Second Coming" and Eliot's "The Hollow Men" would not
be the most often quoted modern poems in the second half of the century, and O'Connor's work would not be so widely read.

My own immediate contribution to O'Connor's apocalyptic thinking
that fall of 1958 was a gift of a paperback edition of Martin Buber's *The
Eclipse of God*, which she received gladly: "I think this book you sent
me is wonderful and I am so very much obligated to you. Buber is a
good antidote to the prevailing tenor of Catholic philosophy which, as
this Fr. Murchland points out in the enclosed reviews, is too often
apologetic rather than dialogic. Buber is an artist" (*HB*, 303). The day
before, she had written this to Father John McCown: "I am reading a
book called *The Eclipse of God* by the Jewish theologian, Martin Buber.
These boys have a lot to offer us" (*HB*, 303). I assume by "these boys"
she meant Jewish thinkers. I had sent her the book with the idea in mind
that Buber's term "the eclipse of God" was more to the point of the
modern world than Nietzsche's term "God is dead," which has a finality
in its ring and with that finality the concept that hardly anyone still living
can grasp even the concept of a supreme being. That it remained a key
term—and I think an unfortunate term—in O'Connor's thought, can be
seen in Richard Gilman's review of *The Habit of Being* in the *New York
Times Book Review*: " 'My audience is the people who think God is
dead,' she writes in 1955."[1] I link the term with another aspect of O'Connor's thinking at this time that disturbed me: her seeming failure to take
into account in her thinking the role of the feminine principle, which as
she herself suggested in a letter to me is found in Buber's dialogic

---

[1] Richard Gilman, "A Life of Letters," *New York Times Book Review*, 18 March 1979,
32.

viewpoint. To me and many others, the Catholic apologetic tone—not to mention the apologetics of Protestant and of other religious and philosophical professionals—seemed to be based on a kind of male chauvinism (I did not know this term at the time, of course), one which handed down great truths from a high position of total male authority. Nietzsche himself was a male chauvinist prophet as were most of the philosophers who followed him, particularly figures like Heidegger and Sartre.

I did not then guess that a man at that time in the department of religion at Emory University, Thomas J. J. Altizer, would in a few years be making Nietzsche's phrase "God is dead" significant in modern theology and even in the mass media. In late fifties and early sixties, Altizer in his classes at Emory and in his writing stressed that Nietzsche's idea was an important one for late twentieth-century humans to consider. By the mid sixties, Altizer had become the most important figure in a new *God-is-dead* school of theology.

I can remember eagerly awaiting my second talk with O'Connor, following her reading of Buber, a meeting that occurred in the late fall of 1958 on my way home to visit my parents. Now on a first-name basis, she met me dressed informally in slacks. Because the weather had turned cold, we sat in the living room under the gaze of her well-known self-portrait with peacock, a work of art which still haunts me and one which helps to explain much about her as both a woman and a Southerner. This remarkable painting reveals a woman who is at once a member of the hierarchy and an artist who is aware of strange and powerful currents of good and evil not perceived by other people. The peacock in the picture is at once the close companion and a bird like Poe's raven who speaks of strange worlds beyond the view of an America still obsessed with material progress. The bird establishes her own preference for nature above the ordinary world and is, finally, a representation of her inner prophetic spirit.

We were soon talking about the modern apocalypse and that subject which was even more important to her than writers and writing: theology. It was an important subject to me also, and I joined her gladly in it; however, I felt that she was not speaking to me in a conversational manner. She made several Nietzschean statements that still stand out in my mind because of their vehemence. One was that 99 percent of people in the world had lost the ability to believe in God at all, and the other was that what was wrong with the Catholic Church was the Irish and that she could say this because she was Irish. Though the two statements were vehement, they had about them a kind of sibylline quality. I agree with Sally Fitzgerald's statement made in an article called "The Andalusian Sibyl" in *Southern Living* that O'Connor was, at times at least, a kind of modern sibyl. Speaking of some of O'Connor's manuscript sheets, Fitzgerald wrote, "Written and rewritten, scratched over, polished, discarded or, less often than not, retained as finally right in their telling, or showing, Sibyl's leaves."[2] Fitzgerald concluded her article comparing the uncomprehending ladies of Milledgeville with women in the original Sibyl's hometown of Cumae: "But then what had the ladies of Cumae thought of the oracular voice not far from their town?"[3]

O'Connor was not, like the Roman sibyl, primarily a person predicting the future, nor was she reared as prophetesses were in ancient Mediterranean civilizations. She did not see herself as a prophet, though she is rightly seen today as a visionary writer. Her mentor, Caroline Gordon, in fact, called her a Blakean visionary when *Wise Blood* was published. O'Connor did have moments in her fiction and in her conversation of truly visionary insight. Thus I remember the *way* she spoke when she told me of her intense concern about the general loss of religious belief. O'Connor's phrasing of the problem deeply impressed me as visionary in nature. But, in most of our long conversation during that second meeting, we spoke in ordinary tones about theology and writing— particularly about how difficult it is to write religious fiction in a time like ours when God, if believed in at all, seems removed from the facts of ordinary life, except of course for a few fundamentalists of the sort O'Connor chose to make leading characters in her best work. Her voice was, in the main, dispassionate. She generally spoke in a serious but matter-of-fact manner with some of the humor and wit she is now known for. But only a few of her sentences were visionary in nature. She was, in some ways, like that type of writer whom Isaiah Berlin called the hedgehog—Tolstoy being the great example—who stand opposed to the fox. The hedgehog has one great truth to communicate as opposed to the fox, who has many little truths he has gathered up. O'Connor's great truth was the one she shared with the three figures she quoted in her first letter to "A," that is, Jung, Nietzsche, and Yeats. In his contemporary biography of Jung, Gerhard Wehr set this truth in the context of modern times:

---

[2]Sally Fitzgerald, "The Andalusian Sibyl," *Southern Living* (May 1983): 65.
[3]Ibid.

And this had to happen at that moment in the historical development of consciousness when, as a consequence of the
rationalism and materialism of extraversion and the conclusion
that "God is Dead," the spiritual dimensions of the depths (but
also the heights!) was lost to a large part of Western humanity.
A religious vacuum had been created, because the traditional
guardians of the religious life had themselves succumbed to the
Zeitgeist, and there was no lack of signals to indicate that the
consciousness of modern man was passing through a zero
point.[4]

The religious vacuum Wehr spoke of was shown by O'Connor in her best
fiction to exist at the heart of many lives. Her greatest fictional talent lay
in her ability to show the human turmoil resulting from the failure of
religious belief. Her great prophetic vision, deeper than any in modern
American literature, concerned the results of God's death (or eclipse) in
terms of an ever mounting tide of criminal violence. An apocalyptic
criminality might be her greatest subject, one she believed should be
written about with intensity.

Louise Abbot and I, along with others, have noted in our meetings
with her the strong sense of O'Connor devoting her whole life to the
labor of proclaiming a vision. But that vision at its deepest is to be found
chiefly in her fiction and not in her conversations or letters. Its profundity
was too great even for her to face it for long; it was ahead of its time.
We are just now catching up to it, understanding something of its meaning.

The part of O'Connor's mind that was traditional and Catholic saw
prophecy as something men uttered. For O'Connor, the roles of men and
women were clearly marked out by the Church. Unlike many American
Catholics in the second half of this century, she saw no repression of
women by the Catholic Church and, if she had lived longer, would have
been plainly horrified at attitudes of many contemporary Catholics as
well as at many changes in the Church after 1970. Thus, on 28 July
1956, O'Connor rapped the knuckles of "A" about her correspondent's
"militant feminism" in connection with the Church:

---

[4]Gerhard Wehr, *Jung: A biography*, trans. David M. Weeks (Boston: Shambaba,
1987) 161.

I observe your Militant Feminist reaction to the Rev. Whatshisname—
only one thing: don't say the Church drags around this dead weight, just
the Rev. So&So drags it around, or many Rev. So&Sos. The Church
would as soon canonize a woman as a man and I suppose has done
more than any other force in history to free women . . . (*HB*, 168).

In spite of believing that the church was the world's greatest force in
liberating women, O'Connor was in fact a certain kind of feminist in
viewpoint, though certainly not a "radical feminist."

In taking the pen name Flannery O'Connor, in moving to New York
to seek a career as a writer, in later establishing herself as an intellectual
speaking and writing on theological and religious matters, O'Connor was
working within an old-fashioned tradition of nineteenth and early
twentieth-century feminism. Possibly the greatest novelist in nineteenth-
century British literature—certainly the greatest woman novelist in all of
British literature—was just such a feminist. This woman was Mary Ann
Evans, who called herself George Eliot. Like George Eliot, O'Connor
believed that she belonged with the best writers and thinkers of her time.
Both writers, however, chose to present their best work under the name
of a man, and both presented in their fiction many of their views through
the voices of male characters. In Dorothea Brooke, the character in her
greatest novel, *Middlemarch*, who is most like George Eliot, we see a
woman who holds up Saint Teresa as her ideal but who can find no way
of achieving such a role for herself in a largely godless society. St.
Teresa was also much admired by O'Connor. For her, St. Teresa was a
woman fully liberated by the Church and by the saintly life that the
Church made possible. Yet George Eliot and O'Connor both believed that
they were sent to address a society that had become so materialistic that
it could no longer deal with the kind of ultimate questions and life solutions that Saint Teresa's life represented for both of them. I think both
women believed that, more than most other writers of their time, they
were addressing significant problems being ignored by essentially materialistic cultures. And both came to believe in their most serious writings
that, both personally and in many of their prophetic characters, they
needed to address the world from a male viewpoint.

Yet what had first interested me most about O'Connor's fiction was
not so much her intellectual abilities combined with a sharp awareness
of social manners, the sort of talents George Eliot had, that is, but rather
the conjunction in her work of the gifts of a twentieth-century George
Eliot with the deep emotional power of an Emily Brontë. In the work

whose title is used for her first collection of short stories, *A Good Man Is Hard to Find*, the author began with a sharp awareness of the details of social life, revealing an irony worthy of Eudora Welty or George Eliot herself; and, when the homicidal maniac called The Misfit is introduced, the tone of the story changes, having become heavily charged with a powerful emotional element not found before The Misfit's appearance. This aspect of O'Connor's writing has been classified by some critics as an example of Southern gothicism and by others, who have in mind her debt to the fiction of Nathanael West, as an example of the absurdist tradition in literature. Both judgments are in part true, but, from my first reading of the story, I saw this element in terms of what E. M. Foster in *Aspects of the Novel* called the "prophetic song."[5] Four novelists, Foster believed, have this profound emotional and visionary quality: Emily Brontë, Melville, Dostoevski, and D. H. Lawrence. This quality is to be found most extensively in O'Connor's second novel, *The Violent Bear It Away*; it is the quality Caroline Gordon called "Blakean" and is seldom seen in any degree in twentieth-century American fiction.[6]

When I first met O'Connor, I was studying her to see how this quality manifested itself in her person. Even from the beginning I noticed what Sally Fitzgerald called her sibylline quality, though this manifestation of her nature appeared only occasionally, possibly in a sentence or two in a single conversation of some length. But the deep visionary quality I found in her writing revealed itself hardly at all. Once, I think, I detected it in a subject that was deeply embedded in her heart—what she described several times to me as the inability of most people to believe in God. When O'Connor spoke deeply about something, it somehow registered in one's mind in such a way that it would remain there for a lifetime. One of these statements for me was that the best letters she received about her work were from criminals. The way she said it was what stayed with me because what she meant, in the very emotional

---

[5]E. M. Forster, *Aspects of the Novel* (New York: Harcourt, Brace & World, 1954) 125.

[6]In a statement originally written for *Wise Blood* but used on the dust jacket of *The Violent Bear It Away*, Gordon stated in part: "This theological framework is near explicit in Miss O'Connor's fiction. It is so much a part of her direct gaze at human conduct that she seems herself to be scarcely aware of it. I believe that this accounts to a great extent for her power. It is a Blakean vision, not through symbol as such through the actuality of human behavior, and it has Blake's explosive honesty."

quality of the statement, was that a confirmed criminal like The Misfit in "A Good Man Is Hard to Find" knew that the destructive side of himself had passed beyond his control and that his fate was due to his inability to believe in any kind of metaphysical realm. To be separated from values based on metaphysical beliefs was for O'Connor a kind of nihilism, a term she used to great effect in her letters. For her, nihilism was everywhere and led straight to some form of criminality. Here then we see the great prophetic element most deeply experienced emotionally by O'Connor—the growing number of "rough beasts" slouching toward Bethlehem to destroy the small city where Jesus came to birth, to wipe out all that remained of the holy in the world.

In conversation and letters O'Connor's prophecy occasionally emerged, but I seldom observed her seeking to yoke in her life and fiction that deeply emotional nature of her prophetic calling to her satiric observations of humans and social decay. For this reason, she is at her top form as a writer in only a few works. The yoking was sometimes present in the fiction, especially in *The Violent Bear It Away*, yet that final novel was itself pointing toward some work of enormous literary power that would next be written. Why it was not to be written is one of the questions that those who love O'Connor's work will always be asking. She was a writer so gifted that her early loss is an American literary tragedy. In two ways I began, as I came to know her better after the first year, to see the personal burden of her own awareness of the growing disintegration of world civilization due to what she believed was the growing inability of modern human beings to retain in their thinking and living the concept of God. Even more, she believed it was difficult for even Catholics to practice the kind of traditional Catholicism that she held to. I must have sensed this in our first meeting because the book I believed then she most needed to read was the one I sent her before our second meeting, Buber's *The Eclipse of God*. Nietzsche's formula "God is dead" was not sufficient for Buber. God, for Buber, was eclipsed because so many people in the twentieth century had willed that eclipse, but for many in the twentieth century the I-Thou relationship was still possible. With my own Protestant and Jewish roots, I felt—if not consciously believed—that a living relationship between a human "I" and a divine "Thou" was being carried on by more people than O'Connor imagined. And I consciously believed then, as now, the Talmudic concept that study, prayer, and service to others are at the heart of true religion, no matter what outward form that religion might take. O'Connor was more dedicated to all three of these activities than anyone I knew at the time, but for her the Church somehow was necessary to validate these activities. Protestants, she told me often, were considered "separated brothers," but in the way she spoke this phrase they seemed very much separated indeed. And yet for her, nearly all Catholics fell short of the kind of religious faith she believed was needed if human existence itself were to continue on the planet. In the South, it was a lonely and painful view to hold, and the view itself helped to account for the inner loneliness her letters reveal.

A strong aspect of O'Connor's prophetic vision was a kind of lamentation that was hard to sustain in the material civilization America was evolving into after World War II. From her perception of a far greater decline in religion than might actually have occurred in her own day sprang an inevitable sadness that her growing acceptance as a writer could not mitigate. Of course, one may well argue that her own religious faith caused her to see literary success as being of no importance, but her anger at bad reviews belies this viewpoint. She was also very much the professional writer deeply concerned with the acceptance or rejection of her work, and what she saw as far too slow a reception of her work by most critics and readers bothered her greatly.

An aspect of her pessimism deeper than her beliefs concerning religion in the modern world sprang from what I believe to be essentially a Southern stoicism adapted even before the Civil War by many of the gentry. After the Civil War, this stoicism, as I will suggest in the chapter that follows on O'Connor and the South, was allied to both a Catholic and Protestant puritanism that found it necessary to repress most aspects of sexuality and most emotions. She was often very critical of attempts to address the subject of sexuality in her works; she had an obvious fear of that side of life which both her stoicism and her puritanism usually caused her to repress. O'Connor was one of our profoundest literary and philosophical critics, but she can be compared with Ezra Pound as described by Ernest Hemingway, who once said of Pound that when his criticism was right he was clearly on the mark but when he was wrong it was extremely obvious. Concerning writers whose works emphasize both the sexual and the emotional aspects of life, O'Connor could be devastating. Of D. H. Lawrence's *Lady Chatterley's Lover*, she wrote to "A": "More pious slop has been written about that book by intelligent people than any other book I can think of" (*HB*, 394). Of Thomas Wolfe, she wrote: "As for R. M.: he is a great admirer of Thomas Wolfe & in my opinion anybody that admires Thomas Wolfe can be expected to like good fiction only by accident" (*HB*, 385). O'Connor's sweeping denunciations of Tennessee Williams, Truman Capote, and Carson McCullers obviously owe much to her revulsion at the frankly sexual in literature.

There was a harshness and an extremism in O'Connor's makeup that she herself was fully aware of. Thus she wrote "A" in 1955: "I am only slowly coming to experience things that I have all along accepted. . . . Conviction without experience makes for harshness" (*HB*, 97). But usually she was not harsh, and, if anything, she underrated the value of her own thinking, which was quite deep and based on careful reading. She also underrated her own best writing, which, even in her lifetime, was having a deeper effect on serious readers than she realized.

I not only emphasized Buber and Judaism in my discussions with her, but I also often brought up Eastern religions and their connections with Christianity. She began by agreeing with me that Christians could learn much from the religions of China and India, but she was, after a time, concerned that I could not be trusted to go very deeply into this subject. In 1961, she wrote to "A" about a book I had sent to her relating Christianity to the East by an Episcopal priest and world-renowned authority on Buddhism, Alan Watts, later known as a hippie guru: "I received of all things two books from Dr. S. this week. One is Alan Watt's *Myth and Ritual in Christianity* which I gather is sort of his current Bible" (*HB*, 451). As one who actively sought heresies and who wrote of creating a character in her story "Parker's Back" who was caught up in heresy, she believed, at least in my case, that it was dangerous to get deeply absorbed in the views of someone not anchored in Catholicism because one might fall into heresy. By this time, my own view was that after three years of friendship in which we exchanged and discussed books—years in which I had read and learned much about Catholicism and related matters—I should have had my viewpoints at least considered without outright and even violent rejection. I could feel by 1961, the year of the low point of our friendship, a growing antagonism to my thought and beliefs. But, by late 1961, for various reasons I will go into more deeply in a later chapter, our friendship took a decided turn upwards. One reason was that we both no longer sought the kind of intellectual struggle we had engaged in with my challenging certain aspects of her peculiarly traditional Catholicism and she challenging views of mine she considered to be heretical. Another reason, I believe, is that she felt—without having thought the matter out—that I was getting too close to certain areas she usually kept locked in her unconscious mind.

I now can see from years of studying her fiction, her essays, and her letters that I was attempting, in seeking to discuss Eastern religion and the work of C. G. Jung with her, to right a balance in her view. It was an attempt to balance the demands of both anima and animus, of feminine and masculine. One of my greatest joys in discovering O'Connor as an intellectual companion was that she had read Jung and understood him, or at least parts of his work. In her copy of Jung's *Modern Man in Search of a Soul*, key passages that show Jung's interest in religion are underlined at length. Three books by Victor White are also in her library with underlinings from *Soul and Psyche: An Enquiry into the Relationship of Psychotherapy and Religion.*[7] Father White, a Catholic priest who worked with Jung and for whose book *God and the Unconscious* Jung wrote a foreword, seemed at the time to be the kind of scholar who could relate the Swiss psychologist's views on the soul and on religion with the doctrines of Catholicism. Looking back now, I believe that White's writing in the fifties helped, along with many other works, to prepare the way for a deeper involvement of the Church with the concept of the feminine. Possibly, O'Connor was already beginning to believe that too great an emphasis on Jung and on depth psychology might lead to the kind of thinking concerning the feminine and sexuality that would bring the sort of changes in the Church, as well as demands still not dealt with, that in fact were made after her death and that would have amazed her.

I could sense in our conversations her growing distrust of Jung and, at the same time, her attempt to link me totally with Jung. I pointed out to her that I did not accept all of Jung by any means and that Buber's *The Eclipse of God* provided an excellent critique of Jung, which I generally accepted. Jung provided a way of righting a balance and—with his concept of individuation—of providing a viewpoint on ways to verify the feminine and masculine elements written on one's soul; he provided a way of balancing, as the Chinese put it, the powers of yin and yang in the individual and in society. Just how much she associated me with Jung and how much she disapproved of this side of my thought and life I did not realize until I read her letters, specifically one to "A" dated 30 April 1960:

---

[7]Arthur F. Kinney, *Flannery O'Connor's Library: Resources of Being* (Athens GA: University of Georgia Press, 1985) 86-91, 28-29.

My Jung friend is not a little bit in love with me but resents me & rather thoroughly I think. Not that the two are mutually exclusive, I just don't think the first is so (*HB*, 394).

She went on to lament that she may have given me "a worse opinion of the Church than he had to start with and this worries me." Quoting someone not named in the letter, she stated that the Church is a " 'divine institution and stands for Christ in the world.' " Then she stated: "[H]e thinks this is sentimentality—whereas all that feminine principle stuff, eros, is a regression to me from what St. Paul means by charity" (*HB*, 394). With the word "eros," she rejected the deepest element in Freud as well as Jung's concept of *anima*, a term which I had urged upon her but which she never adopted. The problem of the two sexes in human affairs was, as I see it in her visionary fiction and in her thought, that the masculine element has clearly overpowered the feminine element, holding it in a kind of dangerous subjection. The problem of the two sexes she brought up early in her correspondence with "A": "What you say about there being two [sexes] now brings it home to me. I've always believed there were two but generally acted as if there were only one" (*HB*, 136). And there is no doubt that this statement in linked to another in the same paragraph: "When I was twelve I made up my mind absolutely that I would not get any older. I don't remember how I meant to stop it. . . . there was something about 'teen' attached to anything that was repulsive to me. I certainly didn't approve of what I saw of people that age" (*HB*, 137). Somehow she managed to dodge the teen years, but this dodging left its mark on her. For instance, her portrayal of teenagers in *The Violent Bear It Away* lacks an authenticity that might have strengthened this important work.

A final point remains to be made about O'Connor as woman and writer, in connection with the male-female dualism. I have said she was an old-fashioned feminist in the George Eliot mold, but what she most missed in her development as a writer who was distinctly feminist in certain ways was a significant encounter with Virginia Woolf and her work. Woolf went a step beyond her own model, George Eliot, by struggling with the great human problem of the balance between anima and animus, of that necessary struggle between the sexes and of the even more necessary achieving, if only for brief periods, some sort of reconciliation between the two principles. For those English writers who struggled with this problem—even Muriel Spark, whom she admired greatly—O'Connor seemed never to have real sympathy, and this might be one reason for a certain narrowness or even puritanism in her writing about relationships between the sexes.

Writing to "A" in 1953 about the authors who influenced her, O'Connor stated: "I read all the nuts like Djuna Barnes and Dorothy Richardson and Va. Woolf (unfair to the dear lady of course). . . . I have read the best Southern writers like Faulkner and the Tates, K. A. Porter, Eudora Welty, and Peter Taylor" (*HB*, 98). It was through the Tates that she learned the most about that subject she could not deal with intellectually, the battle of the sexes. The Tates and the others, except Faulkner, represented a kind of Southern establishment she herself consciously belonged to. Faulkner at his deepest she did not really understand, though she fully appreciated his imaginative power. The irony is that she is the one Southern writer after 1945 who can now be placed in world literature alongside Faulkner. She represents a side of the South the other Southern writers of her generation never came fully to terms with; what that particular South was and is about, and how O'Connor relates to it, we must now examine.

Chapter 2

Flannery O'Connor's South

In her personal and literary preference for Southern writers like Allen Tate, Caroline Gordon, Katherine Anne Porter, Eudora Welty, Peter Taylor, and later Walker Percy, Flannery O'Connor, in her letter to "A" in August of 1955, was stating consciously held beliefs concerning her own background and position in the Southern social scene. All of these writers —and the Vanderbilt Agrarian movement to which several of them were attached—held to beliefs connected with a Southern social establishment which formed many aspects of their literary efforts. Among these beliefs was the concept of a Southern culture that still existed in the twentieth century which was not, as many believed in both the North and the South, so moribund that it could not form the basis for a new literary movement. Allied to this belief was the belief that the South had always had deeper underlying connections with Europe than with the North and that its few significant literary figures—Poe, above all—were aware of both the European sense of social hierarchy and of the European concern with the well-constructed work of art.

The Agrarians above all others—in particular leading figures like John Crowe Ransom, Donald Davidson, Allen Tate, and Robert Penn Warren—held up the ideal of art not so much as a way of self-expression but as a process of "making" artifacts that involved a master-apprentice relationship. To understand O'Connor's South, we must take into account not only her lived experience but, above all, her intertextual and personal literary relationships for the reason that literature from an early age was central to her awareness of the world around her.

Those writers that O'Connor saw as being loosely connected with the Vanderbilt Agrarian tradition, the ones she listed for "A" in 1955, are all distinguished by their opposition to most of the ideas of the first New South movement, as enunciated by the *Atlanta Constitution* editor Henry W. Grady in the 1880s. Grady and his followers advocated the centrality in society of natural science, of education based largely on technology and social science, and of industry. Grady's New South ideas meant the downgrading of the humanities and the arts in both higher and secondary education as well as the exaltation of middle-class commercial and egalitarian ideals over the older religious and hierarchical values of the Old South. Inevitably, the new Southern city—and for Grady his own city of Atlanta—would, in the New South ideology, be supreme over the countryside and its towns, where the older hierarchical values had often held their own even while coexisting, often in the same person or group, with the newer commercial, technocratic ideals. The Agrarians, of course, would be called conservative and even reactionary (and Agrarian leaders like Tate would gladly accept both epithets). But, since 1950, when there has been an increased national awareness of Agrarianism, at least some of the movement's ideas—among them the concern for a regional artistic tradition and the emphasis on ecological concerns—have become part of another "New South."

The second "New South" emerged in the sixties with the civil rights movement. Many journalists and politicians of today who use the term New South are only vaguely aware of Henry Grady's New South ideology that came into being in the 1880s. The second New South is closely connected with feminism and the evolution of black culture. Blacks and feminists both put significant emphasis on their origins, and, since 1960, studies of origins often led black writers to the kind of agrarian and small-town life that is depicted in the most widely read and taught novel by an American black, Alice Walker's *The Color Purple*, a book set in Eatonton, Georgia, a town only twenty miles from O'Connor's Milledgeville. Flannery O'Connor had some of her roots in the Agrarian vision of the South because of her close connections with Caroline Gordon, but, in her search for new visions for men and women of her own age, she was not as different from Alice Walker as it might at first seem when the two are studied together. Later I will discuss Walker's own views of O'Connor and her work.

The search for "roots" by both blacks and feminists is, in fact, similar in some ways to the Vanderbilt Agrarian search for the roots of Southern culture. The black search and the Vanderbilt Agrarian search, different in many ways because of beginnings in two different sets of experiences, both aimed at stimulating new works of literature which would examine earlier group experiences from which contemporary cultures emerged. Another similarity is that women have played a significant role in both black and Agrarian literary efforts in the South. And there are reasons quite similar that make black women and Agrarian women significant figures in the search for cultural roots. One is a close connection with both black and white hierarchical females, in particular those who take a strong interest in recreating the past, particularly individual family heritage. Another is an awareness of practices often associated in America with women—cookery, hospitality, and a concern for propagating the arts.

In her book *Close Connections: Caroline Gordon and the Southern Renaissance*, Ann Waldron describes what she calls the "high point" of the lives of Allen Tate and Caroline Gordon, the summer of 1937 when they were installed at their Tennessee country home named Benfolly: "All the earmarks of their complicated personalities and the elements of what they considered most important—hospitality, a commitment to literature and to young writers, good fun and good food, a classical kind of agrarianism, the knack for living on little money—stand out in brilliant relief."[1] Not only did the Tates plunge into a study of Southern roots, they actually sought to live out the hierarchical past of the plantation. Their attempt was only partially successful, lasting only a few years. As Waldron pointed out, "All the Agrarians, except Allen [Tate] and Andrew Lytle, lived and earned their living in cities. None of them, except Lytle, knew anything about farming."[2]

Tate, however, proved to have little real affinity for the land, and he and Gordon would spend most of their productive lives working either as free-lance writers or as teachers of literature and creative writing, or both at the same time. For them, colleges and universities were essential elements of their life; in fact, they were for most of the Agrarians. A large part of the Agrarians' traditionalism lay in the efforts of Ransom, Warren, Davidson, and both of the Tates to maintain themselves and to help others maintain an active concern not only for the literary tradition of Western culture and for that of the Greek and Roman classics but for the whole of the humanities. To do this, they often found it necessary to attack the continuing incursions of social science into the curriculum of higher education. In their concern more for literary education than for Southern customs, the Agrarians, strangely enough, are not much different from the South's leading black writer, Ralph Ellison, who described in *Invisible Man* his encounter at Tuskegee Institute with the writings of T. S. Eliot and James Joyce. For the Agrarians, as for Ellison, these two

---

[1]Ann Waldron, *Close Connections: Caroline Gordon and the Southern Renaissance* (New York: G. P. Putnam's Sons, 1987) 25.

[2]Ibid., 101.

figures were the essential leaders of the modernist movement of the English-speaking world.

Also like Ellison, most of the well-known Agrarians would suffer from the narrowness of Southern educational institutions and would eventually move north. In 1937, Ransom would find himself at odds with Chancellor Kirkland of Vanderbilt and would leave for Kenyon College in Ohio. As Waldron wrote, "Ransom went to Kenyon College that fall, taking with him, like a Pied Piper, Robert Lowell, Peter Taylor, and Randall Jarrell."[3] In 1938, the Tates found themselves teaching at the Women's College of the University of North Carolina in Greensboro, but in 1939 they went to Princeton University and then on to the University of Minnesota in 1951. The Tates had earlier hoped to be free-lance writers, first in New York and then in Tennessee, but the fact that both were not only writers but people of letters made them more comfortable, in the long run, living and working at educational institutions.

The major Vanderbilt Agrarians made a deep impression on O'Connor because she was like them in many ways. She believed in Southern culture and Southern education, but, even more, she believed in Western civilization and would often view with dismay her own regional culture sometimes unfavorably juxtaposed to the cultural traditions not only of the Midwest and the Northeast but of Europe also. She was a woman of letters, one ready to help younger writers and to advise older ones. She was also concerned with the larger elements of culture, not only those elements based on the humanities but, for her, the deepest element of all, which was religion. Unlike the Tates, who would both become converts to Catholicism in 1947, from her earliest literary efforts she was concerned with religion and its failures in this century. Like the Tates, she saw the writer as Poe had seen him, as one working in both a European and an American tradition, one committed to the entire cultural tradition of the West.

Probably because the South as seen by Caroline Gordon was not so different from the region consciously viewed by the younger Flannery O'Connor, Gordon was quick to see in 1951 the significance of the manuscript of *Wise Blood* that Robert Fitzgerald had sent her. Thus Waldron described Gordon's immediate reaction: "Caroline always said that she knew genius when she saw it. She wrote Fitzgerald that she was quite

---

[3]Ibid., 24.

excited about the manuscript: 'This girl is a real novelist.' "[4] Gordon made some suggestions, which have not survived, and O'Connor, on the basis of them, rewrote *Wise Blood*, and sent it again to Gordon. O'Connor's comments were that Gordon "certainly increased my education thereby." Waldron reported O'Connor's reaction to Gordon's nine pages of comment on the revised manuscript:

> Flannery replied gratefully, saying that she needed all the help she could get. There was no one around Milledgeville, Georgia, she said, "who knows anything at all about fiction (every story is 'your article,' or 'your cute piece') or much about any kind of writing for that matter. Sidney Lanier and Daniel Whitehead Hickey are the Poets and Margaret Mitchell is the Writer. Amen. So it means a great deal to me to get these comments."[5]

Summing up this remarkable example of a mentor-student relationship among women, possibly the most intense in American literature, Waldron stated:

> It was a friendship and a "master class," as Flannery's biographer Sally Fitzgerald calls it, that endured until Flannery's death in 1964. Caroline read and commented on every novel and every short story that Flannery wrote.[6]

O'Connor, however, did not always hold the same views as Gordon on matters of religion or the South, though, like Gordon, she believed in a continuing revision of her writing. She told me once that she took a year to write a short story and that careful rewriting was part of the secret of her success as a short-story writer. I would argue, based on my own conversations with her and a continuing reading of her letters and fiction, that as an insider among the Southern gentry she shared most of Gordon's views, but, as an outsider seeking a path beyond both the Agrarian South and the New South of Henry Grady, she resembled in certain ways someone like Alice Walker.

Caroline Gordon was also for a time Walker Percy's mentor, and he, like O'Connor, was both an insider and outsider in Southern culture. In

---

[4]Ibid., 285.
[5]Ibid.
[6]Ibid.

1951, Percy had sent Gordon a manuscript that was never published and received from her a thirty-page single-spaced letter. " 'It was an extraordinary kindness,' " Percy recalled to Waldron, " 'She told me everything that was wrong with the novel.' " When asked if he took her advice, Percy replied, " 'Not really. . . . The valuable thing was the relationship with her. She had an extraordinary personality.' "[7] Similarly, O'Connor was drawn to Gordon the person, the writer, and the critic without being caught up fully in her vision or her sense of style. Once, in the early sixties, O'Connor told me that Gordon had spent some time visiting her at Andalusia going over her work in detail and suggesting many changes, but she implied that she by no means accepted all of her criticism.

Both O'Connor and Percy—as Gordon herself saw—had gone beyond the Vanderbilt Agrarian vision of the South to discover another, emerging South that would seek to divest itself of the old Protestant narrowness that had accepted slavery and regional fanaticism and hierarchical social relationships. What Gordon gave both Percy and O'Connor was, above all else, a critical viewpoint that took into account the value of their work in terms of the literary currents of the postwar period. She saw, in fact, a new prophetic viewpoint even in their early work, before they had published their first novels. Thus, in 1951, after reading manuscripts by both O'Connor and Percy, she could write Lon Cheney:

> It is no accident, I'm sure . . . that in the last two months the two best novels I've read have been by Catholic writers. . . . The Protestant *mystique* has worn out—but people would have gone on forever writing those curiously dry novels (like Lionel Trilling or . . . Truman Capote) . . . if something new hadn't come along. And Walker's novel and Flannery's novel are IT! They are both so damned good![8]

Nearly thirty years later Lewis P. Simpson would validate Gordon's early judgment of the two Catholic authors. "As committed Catholics," Simpson wrote in *The Brazen Face of History*, "they may be considered eccentrics in a still largely Protestant South; but not only are they the most remarkable Southern fictionists of the past twenty-five years, they

---

[7]Ibid., 284.
[8]Ibid., 285-86.

are pivotal figures in the resolution of the drama of history and memory in Southern fiction."[9] The two were eccentric not so much because of their Catholicism but because they took religion seriously as a necessary factor in both the life and literature of the South and the nation—a factor, they believed, that could eventually help to create a Southern culture far less rigid in its lifestyle. The Protestant mystique, as Gordon had said in 1951, had worn out for all but a few backwoods fanatics, and Catholicism was in her view at least one way that, for a small band of writers in America, England, and France, Christianity could once more be made meaningful in artistic terms.

O'Connor and Percy were eccentric in the South *as Catholics*, but, as Southerners for whom family, hierarchy, and community were vital factors, they were very much a part of the Southern way of life. But O'Connor and Percy were eccentric to both their region and their nation in an even more fundamental way: as modernists they were aware that at least the present form of Western civilization itself was passing away and new life forms were merging that would require some form of religious vision to hold them together. This need for those powers of religion that bind people together, as one historic age comes to an end, is what Simpson meant, I believe, in his statement about these two figures being pivotal in the "resolution of the drama of history and memory in Southern fiction."

The literary and intellectual development of Percy and O'Connor was not the same, but they nevertheless had much in common in their attitudes toward many aspects of the South. In my first meetings with both, they presented themselves as very deeply Southern in their sense of place, of family, and of hierarchy. That is to say, they both were deeply a part of the South and were frank in revealing that part of themselves. But they were also extremely complex people who sometimes presented themselves in somewhat different ways to different people. My own involvement with basic elements of Southern society doubtless made them feel free to be themselves as Southerners who had deep roots in what is traditionally called the Southern "aristocracy" but more correctly should be called the gentry as opposed to at least four other classes—the black gentry, the black proletariat, the white proletariat, and the white yeomanry (with a fifth class being a small black yeomanry).

---

[9]Lewis P. Simpson, *The Brazen Face of History* (Baton Rouge LA: Louisiana State University Press, 1980) 244.

As Southerners with distinct intellectual gifts, they had sought advanced education in the North because the North was traditionally seen by many educated Southerners of the gentry to have superior institutions of higher education. Percy and O'Connor both returned to the South in large part because diseases that made their return desirable, if not necessary. Percy had contracted tuberculosis while dissecting a cadaver as an intern at Bellevue Hospital in New York City. His time in a sanitorium was spent reading philosophy and literature, and he returned to the South and became both a philosopher and a novelist. In 1979, when my wife said to him in a joking manner that if he had gone to Tulane Medical School he might have avoided tuberculosis, he smiled and said something else would have happened. Both Percy and O'Connor seemed destined to have some illness that would force them to at least partially withdraw themselves from ordinary life and to encounter their native Southern culture in its various disintegrating forms. But as intellectuals who were deeply connected with the literature, philosophy, and theology of the Western world, they could leap past a regionalist viewpoint to write for an international audience.

As religionists, Percy and O'Connor could at least conceive of the possibility of cultural renewal because, for them, a religious culture was necessary to sustain and renew culture. Yet, in their work, the sense of disintegration is stronger than the awareness of renewal. This problem, of course, is something O'Connor and Percy both have in common with most of the greatest writers of the South and of modern America. Percy and O'Connor were also similar in their awareness of the Southern social hierarchy and of the place of women in this hierarchy. In Percy's first novel, *The Moviegoer*, the protagonist is fleeing the hierarchical woman, Aunt Emily, who would impose the old ways upon him. Much of Percy's fiction is based on flight, so much so that his work often lacks that sense of immersion in the Southern sense of a particular place that we find in O'Connor's work. The end of flight for Percy is usually a Southern suburb, where the South seems to disappear, but, for O'Connor, the South is mainly a rural, small-town world that is dissolving to make way for the sprawl of the great emerging city. Both Percy and O'Connor looked ahead to a time when the suburb and city sprawls make an end of the old Southern sense of place. Yet O'Connor, like Faulkner and Welty, retains a profound sense of the Southern spirit of place. She spent most of her life in a Southern town, and there she observed many aspects of Southern society in a most profound manner. Her poetic vision was greatly enhanced by this continuing study, which was based as much on a woman's intuition and observation as it was on a dedicated writer's practice of observing all aspects of that life which would provide the raw material for her work.

In my first visit with O'Connor, I particularly observed her Southerner's awareness of the spirit of place. In discussing Faulkner, John Gardner summed up this sense of place as "history, kin connections, identity," and writing of his own western New York, he went on to say: "Perhaps because they were never humiliated by the loss of a civil war, perhaps because their culture is more open to strangers, perhaps for other reasons, western New Yorkers don't feel the same fierce concern about place that traditional Southerners feel."[10] Thus for O'Connor, as for most Southerners up to the recent past, the Southern sense of place included the Southern sense of community, a joining together of Southerners because of past suffering, past humiliations shared, for, among other things, mutual reassurance. But this sense of place and shared experience went back further than the Civil War, as I have pointed out in my book *Revival: Southern Writers in the Modern City*, to the colonial period when the Southern colonies saw themselves as being linked to cities like London and Paris, to the essentially urban-oriented civilization of Western Europe. And although O'Connor's forebears were the Irish of the nineteenth-century immigrations, she shared deeply in the sense of Southern community. This was chiefly because her father's people, the O'Connors, were deeply immersed in the extremely influential Irish segment of Savannah and her mother's people, the Clines, were prominent in the Milledgeville area.

Because both sides of her family had roots in the Southern hierarchy, O'Connor inevitably viewed the South from a somewhat lofty viewpoint, though never from a snobbish one. Robert Fitzgerald has summed up the importance of the Clines in Milledgeville in his introduction to the first edition of *Everything That Rises Must Converge*. Milledgeville itself, he noted, "suggests . . . the strict amenity of the older South, or at least this is what I made of there being so many pillared white houses" (*ERMC*, viii). The Cline house had been the first governor's mansion until that executive home gave way to the nearby antebellum Palladian mansion that today is the home of the president of Georgia College at

---

[10]John Gardner, *On Becoming a Novelist* (New York: Harper & Row, 1983) 26-27.

Milledgeville, formerly the Georgia State College for Women, from which O'Connor graduated in 1945. Peter Cline acquired the original governor's mansion in 1886. He is described by Robert Fitzgerald as a "prominent man, in our American phrase, for many years mayor of the town" who had "married successfully two sisters, Kate L. and Margaret Ida Treanor." Fitzgerald then described the Clines of Milledgeville:

> All of these people were old Georgia Catholics. The first Mass in Milledgeville had been celebrated in the apartment of Hugh Treanor, father of Kate and Ida, in the Newell Hotel in 1847. Mrs. Hugh Treanor gave the plot of ground for the little church that was built in 1874 (*ERMC*, ix).

By the mid-twentieth century, O'Connor's roots in the Milledgeville area were deep and solid. The Clines lived in a town that had once been a major center of culture within the state, one where families still lived who could trace ancestors back to seventeenth-century Virginia and South Carolina.

Considering the long-time emphasis in the antebellum state capital on Protestantism and Anglo-Saxon ancestors, one may well wonder why a Roman Catholic family would be so well received in a bastion of the Old South like Milledgeville. The answer is contained in Robert Fitzgerald's phrase about Peter Cline, that is, that he was a "prominent man, in our American phrase." In the South, as in the rest of America, individuals who could make enough money to establish themselves as a member of the gentry of their particular area were very soon accepted as "prominent." Margaret Mitchell, writing about her mother's Irish family, the Fitzgeralds, shows in *Gone with the Wind* how quickly an Irish immigrant of no means could obtain a large plantation and become in a few years an "aristocrat." Allen Tate, in his biography of Jefferson Davis, revealed that Davis's father was little better than a yeoman farmer with several slaves but that his son could establish himself in only a few years as one of the South's leading patricians.

Yet, in spite of the successes of a family like the Clines, there was always in the rural South a continuing suspicion of Catholics, which did not abate until after World War II. O'Connor's father's Irish family in Savannah had become a solid part of that city's life because the Irish by 1920 were the second largest ethnic group in the city and had made significant contributions to its development. Thus O'Connor's father, as a businessman and a commander of an American Legion post, was well entrenched in a rising middle class that by the time of her birth in 1925 had begun to overshadow in many ways the older entrenched aristocracy.

In her stories O'Connor records the transition in Milledgeville from a once relatively static social order to the predominance of a rising middle class. But when she came to live there permanently in the late thirties due to her father's illness, the old gentry, which included her mother's family, the Clines, was still largely predominant. Yet in even that most conservative area of the state, East Central Georgia, there was always some of the old suspicion of Catholics that had led Georgia in 1928 to vote for Herbert Hoover for president against Al Smith for the simple reason that Smith was a Catholic. The whole of Georgia in the early part of the century was still a part of a social order that was based more on the old agribusiness of the plantation system than it was on the new middle-class commercial and industrial order.

When I first met O'Connor in 1958, she felt deeply that not many of her growing number of readers really understood the essential meanings of her work. Like a European writer who also was a Catholic intellectual, Georges Bernanos, for instance, and like one other Southern Catholic novelist not yet visible in 1958—Walker Percy—she believed that philosophical and theological ideas in fiction should be taken seriously by as many people as possible. But, almost as strong as her interest during that first meeting in my intellectual background and viewpoint, was her interest in my sociological and religious background. She had at once a subtle philosophical intellect and a mind for and an intense interest in subtle differences in social class. Her manner of speaking in a modified Southern drawl with occasional intentional lapses from standard English often put people off who could not see how an authentic intellectual could possibly express herself in the accents and dialect of Middle Georgia. Her manner of speaking was one way she had of maintaining a relationship with as many people as possible in her region, and she early saw me as one who had long been doing much the same thing. Also she so much believed in herself as being part of a particular social order that she was comfortable speaking in the accents of her region of the state, a region she had a high opinion of while seeing all of its faults. She also saw me as one who sprang from practically the same branch of the Georgia gentry as she did and, of course, came from her region. People in Georgia take their localisms very seriously. She also saw that, though I was a "liberal" in a rather academic way for that time, I had a Protestant viewpoint.

Like the good Southerner that she was, she very soon asked me about my hometown of Swainsboro, which she had passed through from time to time. She had college classmates from there. But she quickly made a remark indicating that she had little use for towns like Swainsboro. Such distaste might seem strange considering that Swainsboro had only about 3,000 fewer people than Milledgeville, was nearly as old, and had a social system that was, like many other towns in the state, moving from dominance by plantation aristocracy to middle-class, commercial-industrial control. By the fifties, it was being said everywhere in the state that a town that could not find itself some factories would dry up. But her distaste for Swainsboro, I believe, was based primarily on the fact that before World War II few or no Catholics were to be found in such towns and that Catholicism was anathema to most people in them because of all the prejudices connected with the Protestant Reformation. In contrast, my hometown of Swainsboro in 1940 had several prominent families who were Jewish. One Jew was a member of the city council, and two others owned plantations, one plantation being operated by a Protestant overseer. But, by 1958, Catholics were firmly established in Swainsboro with a church of their own. They were treated like anyone else for three chief reasons: one was that new factories, owned usually in the North, meant that Catholics often would come to work in and even manage plants. Another was that Protestants sometimes brought home Catholic brides after the war. The third and possibly most important was, I believe, that motion pictures with Catholic priests as heroes (*Boy's Town* and *Going My Way*, for instance), along with continuing mass-media pleas for tolerance, had in time made Catholics seem almost like everyone else.

I do not believe that O'Connor ever quite understood how far by 1958 the new tolerance had really gone. Her own viewpoint about religion was based on the immutability of certain basic Catholic beliefs. This she made clear very early in her first conversation with Louise Abbot. "Soon," Abbot wrote about their first meeting in 1957, "though not as soon as I should have expected since it was the subject which interested me most, we got around to religion." On learning that Abbot was an Associate Reformed Presbyterian, O'Connor said, according to Abbot, that "it would probably horrify them to hear it said, still the fundamentalist Protestants and the Roman Catholics were in agreement on many points." She then proceeded to recite the Apostle's Creed as a statement of her own basic Christian belief in order, no doubt, to show that she and a Presbyterian held the same essential beliefs.[11] She said to Abbot, a dedicated Protestant and a writer herself, that " 'I'm no believer in "art for art's sake." If I didn't think I had something to say, I wouldn't write another word.' "[12] Thus, in her conversation with Louise Abbot, she seemed to align herself with the views of one in many ways much like herself, a Southern woman from the area of East Central Georgia, an area very much an entity in itself, self-consciously different in many ways from larger areas of North Georgia and South Georgia. Even the fact that Abbot's hometown of Louisville was, like Milledgeville, a former state capital, gave the two much in common. Louisville had been Georgia's first capital and Milledgeville its second. Yet though she was fully sincere in everything she said to Abbot, O'Connor could be equally sincere in taking a different view of her work and her religion. The different approaches of O'Connor to different people, all of them, I believe, sincere, indicate just how complex a person she was. Like W. B. Yeats, she believed the artist needed many masks in order to survive.

With Richard Gilman, she emphasized the importance of her work as art. In a review of *Mystery and Manners* in *The New York Times Book Review* in 1969, Gilman recalled a note he received from O'Connor after he wrote a favorable review of *A Good Man Is Hard to Find* in the Catholic magazine *Jubilee*. She had thanked him for not discussing her book in "any 'Catholic' perspective." He commented:

> She was especially grateful for that, she told me later when we had become friends. It wasn't that she thought there shouldn't be a Catholic perspective in her work—far from it—but that such a procedure ought to wait until her art was secure, as art. It was extremely important to her that her writing be seen as independent, particularly from any expectations about its moral or spiritual testimony.[13]

In the same article, Gilman also said of O'Connor that "no writer I've known had such devotion to art, felt so much a conduit rather than a source, expected so little beyond internal satisfactions."[14] As a Jewish

---

[11]Louise Hardeman Abbot, "Remembering Flannery O'Connor," *Southern Literary Journal* (Spring 1970): 8-9.

[12]Ibid., 9.

[13]Richard Gilman, "On Flannery O'Connor," *Conversations with Flannery O'Connor*, ed. Magee, 51.

[14]Ibid., 57.

intellectual who had been a Catholic convert and then a lapsed Catholic, Gilman understood both O'Connor's intense devotion to art, defined in *Mystery and Manners* as writing which is "valuable in itself and works in itself," and her profound immersion in what I have suggested earlier is the Catholicism of one, like Eliot, with a traditional mind.

Gilman's description of O'Connor's Catholicism is right to the point as well as is his differentiation of her Catholicism from that of the "tolerant" contemporary American Catholics who seemed to O'Connor to have become so worldly as to have lost the essentials of their religion. ("Is she obsessed with sin?" a worldly nun once asked me, in perplexity, concerning the meaning of her stories.) Thus Gilman wrote: "An intense, unapologetic, and unshakable Catholic, she was for most Catholics who were at all aware of her an agent of something inimical to faith and fatal to moral equilibrium." And he put his finger on what her literary followers like best about her: "[F]or a more sophisticated minority she was a writer of splendor and revelation, which were however often seen more as spiritual than as aesthetic."[15]

Gilman would even spend a weekend with O'Connor and her mother and would, in some of his remarks, go straight to the heart of O'Connor's religious and Southern viewpoints, but, like most critics, he never put the two together very well. The way to understand how they are connected is to see O'Connor in relationship to her mentor Caroline Gordon, who was always the careful artist, always aware of her own mentor, Ford Maddox Ford, and of the critical mind of her husband, Allen Tate. For Gordon, as well as for Tate, the well-made work of art was an act of both religious and Southern piety. The word *piety* might seem suspect when applied to that branch of Southern society to which the Clines and O'Connors belonged. Yet it was a secular piety they all shared, one that had to do with maintaining that dominating hierarchy that Elizabeth Fox-Genovese believes Southern women even more than men created. This piety included the perpetuation of what was essentially an artistic beauty firmly grounded in a European aesthetic (for Gordon, Henry James was the great theorist of the novel) and a social beauty, grounded in European hierarchy, that put courtesy above most other virtues, even higher than religious or civic virtues. O'Connor's elevation of the religious category to a position of highest virtue was atypical of this branch of Southern

---

[15]Ibid., 51.

society and helped to make her, in some eyes, an outsider. Her own visionary power, religious in nature and in a few works down right frightening, made her work, as Gilman has noted, "seem more spiritual" than "aesthetic" to her sophisticated readers. Yet O'Connor, always close to the family and to her Southern location, shared most of the Southern pieties with Caroline Gordon. To know one is to know a lot about the other.

My own connection with a similar branch of Southern hierarchical society, together with a strong interest in literature, myth, and religion, made it possible for me to establish a strong rapport with O'Connor in our first meeting. The same may be said of O'Connor's friendship with Louise Abbot, a woman I had known well before she met O'Connor. The fact that we all three came from East Central Georgia also drew us together. After all, this region, distinctive in itself as I have suggested, had given the world only one "serious writer," Erskine Caldwell, and his work had cast doubt on both Southern hierarchy and Southern tradition. Southerners like Abbot, O'Connor, and I were seeking a consciously developed aesthetic of literature, an awareness of traditional courtesy, and an acceptance of admittedly declining hierarchical values in a Southern literature that would refute Caldwell's trenchant criticism of what to us were only the vague margins of a once rich colonial culture—colonial in relation to Europe, that is, but in 1800 rich, as hierarchical Southerners saw it, in relationship to a Northern culture that would by 1950 be reading the South in terms of Caldwell, Tennessee Williams, and Carson McCullers. It was inevitable that a Southern countermovement to both Southern and Northern critiques of the old hierarchy would arise in the South. The Vanderbilt Agrarians, growing out of the Fugitive movement, were a large part of this countermovement. Gordon rightly saw that the next development beyond the Vanderbilt Agrarians, represented primarily by O'Connor herself and Walker Percy, would deal with the need for a revival of religious support for a way of life that had always had, as Allen Tate had noted, a weak metaphysical underpinning. Yet, as I will continue to suggest, a strong and often hidden aspect of O'Connor's literary vision stands opposed to much contained in the Agrarian viewpoint.

John Crowe Ransom, possibly the most hierarchical of the Agrarians, thought so much of O'Connor that he gladly published her stories in *The Kenyon Review* and even in his old age went about, shortly after her death, giving lectures on her work. With his awareness of aesthetic and feminine beauty, of religious and social ritual, of the need for irony and aesthetic order, Ransom stood for at least one aspect of the hierarchy to which O'Connor belonged. Other individuals of the hierarchy, some rather decadent and proud of their decadence, gave the Northern press from 1865 forward certain images it could use to dismiss what many believed was a culture destroyed by the Civil War. But the Southern hierarchy, often with the help of many Northerners who joined it after 1865, went on struggling to maintain itself, and it brought hard work and a typical American repressive puritanism to this task.

Gilman, for instance, came from New York to visit the O'Connor farm, called Andalusia, a much bigger place than he had imagined, "an expanse of planted fields with a stretch of timberland beyond."[16] Like other Northerners who visited her, he was impressed to find large columned houses, one of which belonged to the Cline family. Andalusia itself was a farm owned and managed by one woman, Regina O'Connor, reported by Gilman to be "a formidable looking woman whom I judged to be about sixty."[17] Gilman noted that all around him lay the material of O'Connor's fiction:

> . . . the leathery, taciturn country people, the hired hands, the mythical elderly ladies we met in town, the dirt roads, the pick-up trucks, Dr. Pepper signs, pentecostal churches. Most central of all was her mother, who enters into so many of her stories as the fulcrum of the violent moral action. There was something larger than life about her, which came, I realized, from her having been transformed in my consciousness into the bearer of aesthetic news. Actually, she was a small, intense, enormously efficient woman, who, as she fussed strenuously and even tyrannically over Flannery, gave off an air of martyr-dom which was the exact opposite of her daughter's quiet acceptance.[18]

In this "enormously efficient woman," as Gilman described Regina O'Connor, we have one of the most important facts of Flannery's O'Con-nor's South. It was the fact of a strenuous and often stoic and puritanical continuing effort since 1865 that had maintained both the agribusiness and industrial enterprises of the Southern hierarchy.

---

[16]Ibid., 53.
[17]Ibid., 52.
[18]Ibid., 56.

Regina and Caroline Gordon were both mentors and living examples for O'Connor. They both spoke to her of the works of that dominant branch of the gentry in which women even more than men, as Fox-Genovese's research shows, created the conditions of the Southern social hierarchy. Regina and Caroline Gordon also spoke continually to the mind and heart of O'Connor about an earlier antebellum glory of the South and the later postbellum need to maintain at least some of the left-over glory and even to push forward into new territory of achievement. Gordon, with her husband Allen Tate and other Agrarians, spoke of the need for a new literature that would not be regional but would have national and even international consequences. Ann Waldron's study of this group's continuing efforts in several areas, but particularly in literature, goes into detail concerning the intensity with which the group worked to create a new Southern literature.

Gilman had come South to visit O'Connor with the usual stereotypes of degenerating Southern "aristocrats" or of Don Quixote planters sipping juleps and living in the past. Instead he met an efficient, formidable middle-aged woman making a living operating a dairy farm of the sort so often described in the daughter's fiction. He could not have known as certain other visitors knew—like myself, Louise Abbot, or William Sessions—how much this mainstream of the Southern "good families" had to struggle to maintain itself and how there had been successes along with failures. Above all, there had been the need to develop an always existing Southern puritanism, not much different from Northern and Western puritanism, one which often repressed the feminine aspects of existence, those most deeply feminine powers found above all in the greatest of the arts.

The Southern gentry had also found it necessary in the postbellum years to compromise with commercial middle-class ideas and ways of life, while nevertheless maintaining, at least up to the time of the civil rights movement, most of its old hierarchical attitudes. Many of O'Connor's struggles with her mother, as we see them both in the fiction and the letters, grow out of the culturally sophisticated daughter's need to take a stand against what she interpreted as her mother's philistinism. Her mother was, of course, like most "successful" Southerners, of good family, a blend of old Southern ideas and new Southern middle-class viewpoints. Louis D. Rubin, Jr. has written that the chief reason why O'Connor turned to fundamentalist Protestants was the need to castigate the comfortable, worldly Southerners like Mrs. Turpin in "Revelation"

who had always "had a little of everything and the God-given wit to use
it right." Of O'Connor, Rubin wrote: "[H]er sympathies lie not with the
prosperous, well-adjusted, comfortable middle-class churches, but with
those who stand outside the respectable community, refuse to accept its
accommodations and compromises, and preach the fire and the plague."[19]
For these fundamentalists, Rubin has reminded us, the Devil is "a real
and tangible presence."[20] This was true also for O'Connor: there were
other worlds that impinged on this natural world of the senses that, in her
art and life, she also celebrated. The impinging worlds were those of
grace and diabolism, and they needed to be taken into account as the
middle class of this century could not take them into account. Yet
O'Connor was not, as I have already said, devoted to the Protestant
cause. Again, it is Rubin who best put his finger on O'Connor's attitude
toward religion:

> It is rather that as a Roman Catholic in the modern South she con-
> sidered fundamentalist Protestantism a manifestation, however grotesque
> and distorted, of a belief in the supremacy of the spirit over the materi-
> alistic ethics and bland rationalism of a "respectable" theology and an
> assertion of true religious identity in a society rapidly losing its sense
> of dependence on God.[21]

Rubin further proved, using Father Gustave Weigel as an example, that
O'Connor's attitude was "not an uncommon one for a Roman Catholic."
But in her own day and much more among our contemporary "tolerant"
Catholics, particularly in America, the easy-going ways of the predominant middle class in religion, as in other activities, have tended to
prevail. O'Connor told me in 1958 that she believed many Catholics did
not really relate in a living way to even the idea of a God of grace.

With her own ideas about the need for a more "fundamentalist"
religious view, O'Connor did not by any means desert all of her mother's
ways. Regina and Caroline Gordon remained the two great mentors in
their different areas. Loxley F. Nichols, who has carefully studied the
mother-daughter relationship as it appears in O'Connor's letters, summed

---

[19]Louis D. Rubin, Jr., "Flannery O'Connor and the Bible Belt," in *The Added Dimension: The Mind and Art of Flannery O'Connor*, ed. Friedman and Lawson, 53.
[20]Ibid.
[21]Ibid., 54.

up the connection between the two: "The letters indicate that O'Connor was perhaps more like Regina than she realized or cared to admit. They also reveal the ambivalence of O'Connor's regard for her mother."[22] Thus we see an O'Connor who is both an insider and an outsider in accepting and rejecting at the same time a place in a Southern ruling class that was becoming everyday more middle class and commercial in order to maintain its local authority as well as a vital relationship with the rest of America. But there was, along with her well-stated minority view on religious practice in the modern world, another way in which she was an outsider: she was a woman of letters. Once I had suggested to her that she was becoming, even in her thirties, a woman of letters, but she frowned at the term. Yet, the next time I saw her, she spoke in a pleasant manner about the idea of eventually becoming a woman of letters, possibly one like Caroline Gordon. Later, in 1960, I had a significant dream about her; in the dream, she was a middle-aged woman of letters, well-dressed and magisterial, as she was capable of being even in her thirties. In one aspect of the dream, O'Connor kept part of herself locked in a closet: that side was Carson McCullers. I hesitated to tell her the dream; when I did tell it to her, she did not speak but smiled slightly as if in assent. If O'Connor had lived into her fifties, I think she would have been the most influential woman of letters that Southern literature has ever had because of her great appeal to younger writers throughout this country and most of Western Europe as well.

O'Connor was too strong by far in her fanatical denunciations of writers like Carson McCullers, Truman Capote, and Tennessee Williams not to be caught up unconsciously in some of their views. They too helped to form her intellectual and critical outlooks even though she could not admit it. She was consciously, in part at least, at one with Agrarians like Tate and Gordon, but she was also in revolt against a gentry that could never acknowledge how much it had ignored the plight of blacks and poor whites, of women and immigrants. Her fiction reveals a concern with outsiders that is as great as any in the work of McCullers or Williams. Virginia Spencer Carr has written of McCullers that she was often reminded as a child that "she was different, somehow, an entity set apart from any group," and that McCuller's "identification with the alien, poor, and oppressed evolved as a natural accompaniment to such

---

[22]Loxley F. Nichols, "Flannery O'Connor's 'Intellectual Vaudeville': Masks of Mother and Daughter," *Studies in the Literary Imagination* 20/2 (Fall 1987): 25.

feelings."[23] There were few sensitive, intelligent Southerners of O'Connor's age who did not have the kind of feelings just described by Carr. The chief concern of the Agrarians was to defend what was good about Southern culture and to promote the development of a branch of modern literature that would be truly Southern, but their views about the plight of blacks and other outsiders did not take into full account the suffering of these groups in a hierarchical South.

The stern caste system of race before 1960 made it hard for sensitive people who disliked the caste system to live in the South, unless they were attached to one of a few liberal Southern universities or were living in one of three or four Southern cities that contained large groups of liberals. O'Connor would probably not have gone to Iowa and then to New York to find herself as a writer unless she had in some ways at least sought to break with certain aspects of the South which later, as a writer in the South, she accepted with only a mild liberal protest.

O'Connor's South was thus a place that she could depict in her fiction as a region with many human injustices, but, in her conscious view of the South, influenced as it was increasingly by Caroline Gordon and other Agrarians, she could see a place where deeper human relationships were generally possible for her than she had found in the North. As Sally Fitzgerald wrote, "[I]t is clear from her correspondence that she cherished her life there [in the South] and knew that she had been brought back exactly where she belonged and where her best work would be done" (*HB*, xvi).

The South was also a place that provided her with material for her writing, the act of which was the dominant fact of her everyday life. What chiefly kept her fictional South from being like the South of Gordon and the Vanderbilt Agrarians was that she was of a different generation than the Agrarians, and she had a mind informed by different works of literature and philosophy from the continent of Europe. She was possibly the one Southern writer of this century who had developed a natural gift for thought along the lines of various secular and religious minds of France and Germany. Out of what amounted to a long self-taught course in philosophy and theology came a critical view of the novel that undergirded most of her writing. Only since her death have we been able to grasp the depth of her thinking. It is now necessary to look

---

[23]Virginia Spencer Carr, *The Lonely Hunter: A Biography of Carson McCullers* (New York: Carroll and Graf Publishers, 1985) 23.

at that overall set of concepts that guided her mature thinking and, after that, to look at her own particular practice of literary criticism. Yet it always is necessary to see her intellectual life in the context of her life in the South. Of the many Souths that exist for Southern writers, hers was one of the strangest and most profound: this strangeness and profundity sprang primarily from her powerful literary imagination.

II.
The Thinker

Chapter 3

The Intellect of the Southern Writer

In 1969, Richard Gilman remembered Flannery O'Connor as one who "suspected that she didn't know the intellectual world, and was aware that it had its suspicions of her."[1] Gilman added that she "was extremely firm in almost all her judgments and possessed nothing of what we like to call an 'inquiring' mind," though he reported later in the same interview that she did inquire about the way Norman Mailer and other New York writers "acted and lived."[2] Gilman's explanation for O'Connor's failure to have an "inquiring mind" was that "her illness had put her up against the wall, so that being interested in anything that wasn't fiercely to her purpose in the small space she had to operate in was a rare luxury." He quoted her, to back up his judgment, to the effect that a writer needs "a certain grain of stupidity."[3] Although his insights into O'Connor's life and art are often extremely perceptive, Gilman in his interview failed to grasp the kind of literary and philosophical mind O'Connor possessed. This was due to the fact that she at times hid her deepest thoughts from some people. But it is also due to a viewpoint that seems to have cut her off from many intelligent readers, even while this same mind and sensibility draws to her work one of the largest cults in contemporary literature.

The publication in 1979 of her letters and the earlier publication in 1969 of her occasional prose, much of the best of which first appeared as addresses to various college groups, made it clear to the growing number of her readers that O'Connor had well thought-out positions on the art of fiction as well as on many other subjects. Any careful reader of her letters and of *Mystery and Manners* can see quite clearly that she was thoroughly an intellectual, one who was widely read and one who had spent much time thinking through the positions she would take in essays and speeches, particularly on the subject of fiction, but also on what she

---

[1]Richard Gilman, "On Flannery O'Connor," in *Conversations with Flannery O'Connor*, ed. Magee, 55.
[2]Ibid., 54-55.
[3]Ibid.

considered to be the major problems of the age. Yet many modern intellectuals inevitably find it difficult to understand her overall critique of modern life. As late as 1979, a reviewer in the *Atlantic* wrote that she was "puzzling to the critics."[4]

Robert Coles felt it necessary in his *Flannery O'Connor's South* to try to make it clear how she differed from "the intellectuals," meaning, as he put it, the secular intellectuals, thinkers who are not, as O'Connor was, theological thinkers. Coles noted, and her letters make it clear, that she shared the concerns of those secular intellectuals who supported the civil rights movement. The letters make clear that she supported the work of Martin Luther King, Jr. and that she voted for John F. Kennedy in 1960. Yet Coles stated why many "secular intellectuals" dislike O'Connor or even find her thought impossible to understand: "The secular messianic mentality was not hers . . . she mocked it—a critically important element in her writing."[5] But it is always necessary to emphasize, even more than Coles does, that, though she opposed modern messianic utopianism because for her it denied the role of grace in human existence, she nevertheless maintained a mildly liberal viewpoint that was linked to a kind of social critique of both the South and of America. This critique is to be found in her fiction, but, in her conscious mind, it is not, in its depths, fully present. Between O'Connor the artist and O'Connor the thinker there was sometimes a gap, the sort of gap one often finds in great artists.

O'Connor in her early career, beginning even with the five years of the writing of *Wise Blood*, possessed three distinct intellectual viewpoints, all of which were linked to her life as a writer in the South who took being Southern very seriously while at the same time, rightly as it turned out, seeing herself as a writer for all of America and for all of that civilization which can be called Western. One of O'Connor's many viewpoints is that viewpoint often associated with other Southern writers of her own period, writers like Carson McCullers, whose work she detested but with whom she is often linked by people only vaguely familiar with her work; it is a viewpoint, found in all of her best fiction, that takes into full account the suffering endured by most women, children, and blacks in a Southern culture whose hierarchy had become, after the Civil War,

---

    [4]"Short reviews," *Atlantic Monthly* (June 1979): 96.
    [5]Robert Coles, *Flannery O'Connor's South* (Baton Rouge: Louisiana State University Press, 1980) xxvi.

extremely rigid, but one also that was, by O'Connor's time, becoming a middle-class urban way of life. This viewpoint I will analyze at length when I take up O'Connor's fictional vision, particularly as it is found in *Wise Blood* and her best stories. Why she did not in full consciousness grasp all of the implications of this particular viewpoint in intellectual terms—that is, why she never went beyond the mild liberalism she adhered to—can be seen in the fierceness with which she held to three other dominant intellectual positions.

These three positions—that of Southern Agrarianism, of a strictly orthodox Thomism, and of an apocalyptic Catholicism—she often held with fierceness because, for one reason, these positions were either ignored or attacked by the secular intellectuals she either did not understand or who did not like her work. For her, the American capital of secular intellectualism was New York, a city she had ambivalent views about. But it was not a city she disliked in the manner of many Southern conservatives. After all, she had gone to New York to make a name for herself as a writer, and she would always express an interest in it, as she did to Richard Gilman in her concern with understanding the intellectual and literary life of the city. Once she even told me she wished she was living again in New York City, even in Greenwich Village. Life on a farm as a writer, which she often felt suited her exactly, was also a place where she seemed to herself at times somewhat cut off from the mainstream of contemporary culture. When I told her about seeing Fellini's *La Dolce Vita*, for me the great motion picture of the sixties, she seemed entranced, later writing "A" that "He was full of *La Dolce Vita*" and "He thought it was a great movie. Have you seen it?" (*HB*, 459). And yet the seriousness with which she took her calling—I might even say the burden of her task as both thinker and writer of fiction and occasional prose—drove her to work so hard and think so deeply that I believe she needed more of what for her would have been a lightness of touch that might have come from being involved in the everyday life of other contemporary writers. Our first conversation contained literary gossip, and she enjoyed a certain amount of both literary and Church gossip with several correspondents, as her letters indicate. Gossip for O'Connor was, as far as I could tell, not usually an opportunity for malice but was a way of letting off steam, of relaxing from the cultivation of various unpopular ideas that nearly all mainstream American intellectuals did not take into account as meaningful for contemporary culture.

Before discussing her deepest ideas about life, it is first necessary to see how her religion and her Agrarianism were linked with the life she shared with her mother on the dairy farm. The view of Regina O'Connor that I and other Southerners who knew her had was far different from Gilman's view of her as a kind of tyrant, though I think everyone who observed her would have agreed with his word *formidable*; and she was, as he suggested, both hardworking and efficient as a dairy farmer. She also was, as he did not really observe, very much the Southern lady of a good family of Middle Georgia, which meant she was never snobbish, never condescending, always polite, strong in her opinions but never overbearing.

Mary Barbara Tate, an associate professor emerita of Georgia College at Milledgeville and a founder and editor of *The Flannery O'Connor Bulletin*, has given us an account of the author as she presented herself to a book club she organized in 1956 that included Caroline Tate and her husband and several others, a club that met once a week for three years, reading an "assigned" book each week for discussion. The meetings went on at Andalusia for about three hours, and O'Connor fully participated in them and socialized freely with everyone. Mary Barbara Tate's remarkable article demonstrates why impressions of Northern intellectuals like Gilman, though often showing correctly several sides of the author, do not reveal either a large part of her intellectual nature or of her sometimes playful and socially developed side. Tate's explanation concerning this side of O'Connor, a side that was seldom exposed to interviewers or to others who did not know her well, is that she cultivated a "pose," a fact I gradually became aware of after a year of correspondence and several long conversations. Thus Mary Barbara Tate wrote: "Her pose, for which I have no documented explanation, as a 'country girl,' ignorant of modern fiction and poetry before her studies in Iowa has always intrigued me."[6] Tate pointed out that O'Connor received an excellent education at Georgia State College for Women. I agree with Tate's reason for O'Connor's pose: Southerners, she explained, are so often treated as "ignorant and backward" in other parts of the country that they, like many blacks all over America, have played roles in order to avoid humiliating comments. Thus Tate, having experienced this kind of humiliation herself while living outside South, wrote: "I am convinced that

---

[6]Mary Barbara Tate, "Flannery O'Connor at Home in Milledgeville," *Studies in the Literary Imagination* 20/2 (Fall 1987): 34.

Flannery, too, heard derogatory remarks often, and I think that she disarmed criticism rather weakly by alleging her own lack of solid education and literary studies."[7]

The various sides of O'Connor's life and intellect must be taken into account if we are to understand both her intellectual viewpoints and her vision, which contained insights and ideas she did not always consciously grasp. The Thomist side of O'Connor, with its sense of order, has been related by several scholars to the Vanderbilt Agrarian side with its hatred of abstractions and its demand for imaginative literature that grows out of what Coleridge called the "I am." No critic has dug as deeply into this side of O'Connor's intellectuality as Marion Montgomery has in his 1,300-page trilogy, *The Prophetic Poet and the Spirit of the Age*, of which his first volume, nearly 500 pages long, is about O'Connor: *Why Flannery O'Connor Stayed at Home*. Using the philosophical works of Eric Voegelin, a German philosopher O'Connor read but never got very deeply into, Montgomery pointed out how much of her work is, in one sense, an attack on what Voegelin called secular gnosticism, a form of thought which denies being, thereby, in Montgomery's opinion, leading to an "intellectual egocentricity which increasingly denies power in the world beyond that which the mind may itself generate." Montgomery summed up Voegelin's formula concerning secular gnosticism by quoting the German philosopher: " 'Gnosis desires dominion over being.' "[8] Or, to put this into a formula Montgomery is fond of, secular (or modern) gnostics seek to divinize man and to humanize God.

Walker Percy has said much the same thing as Montgomery about modern gnosticism in his essays and fiction, and O'Connor felt a great affinity for Percy. But what makes O'Connor both a profounder thinker and artist than Percy is the complexity of her intellectual and visionary makeup, which in part is expressed in what I have called the outsider-insider aspects of her life. She had strong emotions on both sides of the fence. The outsider as a modern Southern Catholic, an old-fashioned Thomist Catholic, and a Vanderbilt Agrarian must be seen in juxtaposition to the troubled insider struggling, often unconsciously, with the agony of the Southern past and present. She felt outsider alienation as a woman, a Southerner, and as a writer-intellectual in a Philistine society,

---

[7]Ibid.

[8]Marion Montgomery, *Why Flannery O'Connor Stayed at Home* (La Salle IL: Sherwood, Sugden and Company, 1966) 46.

which included her mother's own house. Her outsider qualities are also to be seen in her religious visionary nature seeking expression in a church still based on the rationalistic philosophy of Aquinas, which she accepted. Yet she was, for most Catholics, an outsider, too sweeping in some of her conclusions as outsiders are likely to be, but there is no doubt that the emotions of the religious outsider gave fuel to her best work. The fiery Protestants in her fiction are themselves outsiders among both the fundamentalist and middle-class Protestantism.

The disquieting energies of the outsider can be seen in O'Connor's first important work, *Wise Blood*. Her Protestant protagonist, Hazel Motes, remains alienated from all other religionists. The first critic to explore the depths of O'Connor's alienation was Stanley Edgar Hyman in his comparative analysis of Nathanael West's *Miss Lonelyhearts* and *Wise Blood*. In comparing the two, he showed the value for both writers of their multiple alienation:

> As a writer she had the additional advantage, as West did, of multiple alienation from the dominant assumptions of our culture: he was an outsider as a Jew, and doubly an outsider as a Jew alienated from other Jews; she was comparably an outsider as a woman, a Southerner, and a Roman Catholic in the South.[9]

I would go beyond Hyman by indicating that O'Connor was at once at home as a Southerner, a Catholic in the South, and as a woman and a professional writer and, *at the same time*, was not at home in any of these roles. But as a great artist and a powerful thinker, she could hold opposite attitudes in tension and could live out Yeats's belief that out of our quarrels with others we make rhetoric and out of our quarrels with ourselves we make poetry. Her ambivalent attitude toward the South is more common than might be imagined. I remember when Samuel Holt Monk, a noted scholar of eighteenth-century literature, who was Allen Tate's close friend and office mate at the University of Minnesota, said in 1953, "When I'm up here I want to be down there, and when I am down there I want to be up here." And yet in spite of her ambivalence, it was quite true that, as Sally Fitzgerald wrote, "it is clear from her correspondence that she cherished her life in the South" (*HB*, xv). Like

---

[9]Stanley Edgar Hyman, *Flannery O'Connor* (Minneapolis: University of Minnesota Press, 1966) 46.

Gordon and Tate, O'Connor believed there was still a culture in the South that could sustain the creative writer.

Flannery O'Connor, then, contrary to Montgomery's title, *Why Flannery O'Connor Stayed at Home*, did not entirely stay at home. Her time in Iowa, New York, and Europe was limited to only a few years, but in her mind she was, for instance, often in France with Georges Bernanos and François Mauriac. The book that more than any other she pressed upon me to read was Bernanos's *The Diary of a Country Priest*, and I read her own copy. She noted with satisfaction to "A" about her efforts on behalf of Bernanos: "I have introduced him to Bernanos whom he likes. Do you know any Catholic crisis theologians? Only crisis theologians seem to excite him. He has a very fine mind in spite of the apocalyptic tastes" (*HB*, 302). Strangely enough, she became for me the most apocalyptic modern writer I have ever encountered. Bernanos's novel mirrored her own sense of cultural and religious impoverishment in her native region, dealing as it does with a poor, dying priest who finds little help or understanding among either his own parishioners or his fellow priests. By insisting that I read Bernanos's best novel, she seemed to say to me, here we see in Bernanos's poor priest the lot of one seeking a larger spiritual vision. Yet her own local culture in Savannah and East Central Georgia, she believed, gave her much, and she defended that culture. In spite of a generalized cultural poverty that everyone in the modern world shares—in France as in Georgia—she also partook of a local, regional, and national culture, so much so that she became a literary light for her entire nation. Thus I can agree with Sessions's statement about her use of and delight in her local world: "She grew up in a society that could distinguish, or for that matter, discriminate. With this gift, all the degradations of Hazel or Hulga or their brothers and sisters could be placed in reference to some communal pervading reality."[10]

Part of O'Connor's communal reality was the sense she developed early in her reading of Poe and Hawthorne that literature springs primarily from an intertext. This basic intertextual proposition she stated quite clearly in her most influential essay, "Some Aspects of the Grotesque in Southern Fiction": "I think the writer is initially set going by literature more than by life" (*MM*, 45). She also stated that the "Southern writer is forced from all sides to make his gaze extend beyond the surface, beyond

---

[10]William Sessions, "A Correspondence," in *The Added Dimension*, ed. Friedman and Lawson, 211.

mere problems, until it touches that realm which is the concern of prophets and poets" (*MM*, 45). She was, of course, speaking for writers like herself and not for most other Southern authors. Of those writers having such a worldview, only Walker Percy could really be put along side her, as Gordon saw would eventually be the case when she first read their manuscripts. Percy made more use of speculative philosophy than did O'Connor, but both writers drew in their best work from prophets, both modern and otherwise. And the result for both was the kind of poetic and prophetic fiction that O'Connor believed the best Southern writing would become. Thus far, no other writers in the South have followed O'Connor and Percy into the kind of vision that is contained in their work, although it is true, as she predicted, that fiction would move into a more prophetic and poetic mode.

By the beginning of the fifties, with William Styron's *Lie Down in Darkness* in 1951 and Ralph Ellison's *The Invisible Man* and O'Connor's *Wise Blood* in 1952, a new period of Southern fiction that was in fact both poetic and prophetic began to emerge. Also in Styron, O'Connor, and Ellison could be seen what she would call concentration and distortion: "His [the writer's] way will much more obviously be the way of distortion" (*MM, 42*). What she meant by distortion was a form of expressionism, the kind of absurdist techniques that emerged particularly in French drama after World War II. For that reason, as she stated in some of her occasional prose, we should not view her fiction as primarily realism, even though it does contain brilliant realistic scenes. For her, the essential vision was the chief aspect of her work; she believed the novelist must be characterized by vision, not function. But what is this vision, if it is not essentially apocalyptic? The title that the Fitzgeralds selected for the collection of occasional prose, *Mystery and Manners*, sums up for many the essence of O'Connor's fiction. Mystery is indeed invoked in her work. Joseph Campbell wrote that one of the functions of myth is to put human beings in touch with the realm of mystery but that another is to depict the holy, the element of the sacred, as Mircea Eliade called it. This element, Eliade noted, often exists side by side with the profane. A profane world inevitably cries out for new visions of both mystery and a sense of the sacred. And O'Connor believed by 1960 that the entire world was ripe for a new apocalypse, a vision, that is, of the juxtaposition of the sacred and the profane.

What made apocalypse inevitable for O'Connor was her belief that God for most people was dead. This "death" made the coming of Yeats's rough beast inevitable, and O'Connor could even write in her first letter to "A" that her stories report the "progress of a few of them [rough beasts]" (*HB*, 90). But apocalypse as a concept means more than the destructive upheaval of one world; it means also the emergence of a new and better world based on new visions of the sacred. In turning to the work of Teilhard de Chardin for inspiration, she was seeking late in her life to find a visionary basis for a new age in which there would be a renewal of the sacred. The title of her second, posthumously published volume of stories, *Everything That Rises Must Converge*, is taken from Teilhard's *The Phenomenon of Man* and suggests that, as people rise spiritually through grace and the love that results from it, convergence into a new social order will result. Most of the stories in this second volume depict a failure of characters to rise spiritually, but at least three of the works, "Revelation," "The Enduring Chill," and "The Lame Shall Enter First," point to possibilities of a continuing growth leading to a "convergence" between people. O'Connor's vision of convergence conveys both her spiritual sense of new life and her desire for a new and just social order.

Although O'Connor herself sometimes appeared to draw back from the full implications of the meaning of apocalypse, Walker Percy credited her with being a truly apocalyptic novelist. In his essay "Notes for a Novel about the End of the World," Percy defined apocalypse in effect as "the end of the world—i.e., the passing of one age and the beginning of another."[11] For Percy, the chief task of the "Christian novelist" is to deal with this passing of an age even though he is saddled with "a discredited Christendom" and a "defunct vocabulary." The way for Percy lies in the method of Joyce's Stephen Dedalus: "[H]e calls on every ounce of cunning, craft, and guile he can muster from the darker regions of his soul."[12] His example of a writer who performs in this manner is O'Connor:

Flannery O'Connor conveyed baptism through its exaggeration, in one novel as a violent death by drowning. In answer to a question about

---

[11]Walker Percy, *The Message in the Bottle: How Queer Man Is, How Queer Communication Is, and What One Has to Do with the Other* (New York: Farrar, Straus, and Giroux, 1979) 114.
[12]Ibid., 118.

why she created such bizarre characters, she replied that for the near-
blind you have to draw very large, simple caricatures.[13]

In taking into account O'Connor's expressionistic distortion in *The Violent Bear It Away*, Percy failed to note that the author does not through
"exaggeration" speak to very many of the blind. This novel remains her
most difficult because it is drawn from what Percy, referring to Stephen
Dedalus, called the "darker regions of his soul." Apocalyptic writing is
often "dark," beyond ordinary comprehension, yet, as in the case of the
poetry of Yeats and Eliot, there is a power that lures the reader to it in
spite of his or her incomprehension.

O'Connor and Percy both made efforts to clarify their apocalyptic
views, O'Connor in her use of Teilhard to suggest the possibilities of a
new age and Percy, for instance, in the epigraph to his second novel, *The
Last Gentleman*. Percy, interestingly enough, used for the epigraph a
quotation from O'Connor's favorite modern Catholic theologian. Taken
from Romano Guardini's book *The End of the Modern World*, Percy's
epigraph is at once an acknowledgement of the end of modernism and of
the attendant pains to accompany the certainty of a better age to follow:
"[W]e know that the modern world is coming to an end. . . . the world
to come will be filled with animosity and danger, but it will be a world
open and clean." In his novels of the eighties, *The Second Coming* (1980)
and *The Thanatos Syndrome* (1987), Percy sought to picture the possibilities of a new world, but his sense of the dangers existing in the old
world loom much larger. In both books the dying forms of twentieth-century Christianity are roundly attacked, and in each book there exists an
authentic Christianity, whose few followers are in hiding from modern
"religion." At the end of *The Thanatos Syndrome*, a doctor uses Jungian
psychology to help a woman find herself. The one Catholic priest in the
book sustains himself by drinking and hiding most of the time in a forest.

O'Connor, on the other hand, turned away from her study of Jung
and other depth psychologists in order to suggest the possibilities of a
new age emerging even in our own second half of the twentieth century.
As one of the profoundest commentators on O'Connor's apocalyptic
visions, Joyce Carol Oates, has written:

---

[13]Ibid.

Like Teilhard, O'Connor is ready to acquiesce to the evolution of a
form of higher consciousness that may be forcing itself into the world
at our expense. . . . Man cannot remain what he is. . . . We are confronted, says Teilhard, with two directions and only one upward and the
other downward.[14]

In spite of the profundity of her own vision of O'Connor's apocalypse,
Oates did not put Teilhard in the proper perspective in her assessment of
O'Connor's worldview. The French paleontologist's vision she discovered
relatively late in her development. It was an attempt, in my opinion, to
right the balance of her own pessimism concerning the human condition,
a pessimism that grew out of too deep a concentration on the dark side
of her apocalyptic Catholicism. To fellow Catholic Cecil Dawson, she expressed her own pessimism concerning Catholicism in America: "I know
what you mean about being repulsed by the Church when you have only
the Jansenist-Mechanical Catholic to judge it by." In the same paragraph,
however, she stated that "Catholicity has given me my perspective on the
South" (*HB*, 230). Yet her Catholic worldview was based on her discovery of certain continental novelists, philosophers, and theologians:

> Anyway to discover the Church you have to set out by yourself. The
> French Catholic novelists were a help to me in this—Bloy, Bernanos,
> Mauriac. In philosophy, Gilson, Maritain and Gabriel Marcel, an Exis-
> tentialist. They all seemed to be French for a while and then I discover-
> ed the Germans—Max Picard, Romano Guardini and Karl Adam (*HB*,
> 231).

From my own conversations and correspondence, I came to believe that
the two most important writers for her, among the above, were Picard
and, as I have already suggested, Bernanos. Picard, a Swiss Jewish thinker who is hardly known at all in this country, gave her a key image with
which to fashion her own apocalyptic worldview, one for her more fruitful than Nietzsche's death of God image. This image is contained in the
title of Picard's key book, *The Flight from God.*

Picard's central concept is that modern man is in a kind of mass
flight and that this flight leads to the "great city." "The great city," Picard

---

[14]Joyce Carol Oates, "The Visionary Art of Flannery O'Connor," in *Flannery O'Connor*, ed. Bloom, 52.

wrote, "is the place of meeting for those who flee." People meet in this archetypal city, an urban area that Oswald Spengler called the megalopolis, in order to "take lessons from one another for the Flight."[15] People in Picard's book are much like those in the city of Albert Camus's *The Fall*, where modern man fornicates and reads the newspaper: "Again people sit in the cafes and appear to do nothing but read newspapers and gossip. But each one regards his fellow with suspicion."[16] In the Flight, nature itself is destroyed to make way for the total domination of the City: "The heavens seem empty, as though everything in them had been swept away by the stream of the Flight." The seasons themselves "no longer keep faith with each other. No longer does one season trust another. As though on the eve of a great catastrophe, everything is dissolved, in dread, ready to speed away in the Flight."[17] In Picard, we encounter a sense of the absolute collapse of an old order that is found in all apocalyptic literature, yet there is also a suggestion, as in the great apocalyptic vision at the end of Dostoevski's *Crime and Punishment*, of a small number of hidden people who keep the faith and wait for a time beyond the Flight. The end and the beginning are the central concepts in Picard's book, and he said as much himself early on: "One advances to the very end of being, towards eschatology, for the eschatological is the last frontier."[18]

O'Connor's sense of the city in her fiction is based firmly on Picard's vision of the flight from God, and the great city is the most important sociological and eschatological fact in her work. In her fiction people are either leaving a desecrated countryside to go to the city or else they are leaving the city to carry their flight out into the country. And here we are at the heart of both the intellectual worldview and the poetic vision of Flannery O'Connor. As critics have inevitably pointed out, she was a Thomist who literally read St. Thomas almost every night and an Agrarian who accepted quite consciously ideas received from Gordon, Tate, and Ransom. I have sat upon her porch and heard her quote these three Agrarians and St. Thomas as well, speaking as she often did in terms of a Catholic and Southern hierarchical order that existed in the mid-

---

[15]Max Picard, *The Flight from God*, trans. Marianne Kuschnitsky and J. M. Cameron, intro. Gabriel Macel (Chicago: Henry Regnery Co., 1951).
[16]Ibid., 177.
[17]Ibid., 178, 180.
[18]Ibid., 35.

century. But O'Connor the outsider had, under the cover of a worldview inherited from thinkers like Aquinas or Tate, erected another worldview, put together from apocalyptic thought and art that depicted man's flight from God and his encounter with the diabolical principle. The link between Picard's "flight" and the diabolical is in fact made by Gabriel Marcel in his introduction to the English edition of *The Flight from God.* In assessing Picard, Marcel, who knew him personally, wrote that "we are dealing . . . with a visionary not a philosopher." Marcel spoke of "Picard's metaphysics of Flight, which personally I should prefer to call perdition."[19] O'Connor herself began her basic intellectual work in order, as she put it in a letter to Dawkins in 1957, to discover the Church by herself. Her philosophical and theological views served as a springboard into a vision that was beyond any thing she could find in the thinkers that she read.

As a philosophical thinker herself, O'Connor inevitably was drawn to religious existentialists like Buber and Marcel, particularly Marcel, who as a Catholic existentialist also influenced Walker Percy. Marcel's most original concept is one that he called intersubjectivity, a more significant concept for him than Kierkegaard's subjectivity because, as Marcel believed, only through interrelationships that are loving can humanity break the chains of isolation that bind it in this century. O'Connor's friend Brainard Cheney in 1964 in The *Sewanee Review* noted that *Wise Blood* is in effect a parody of atheistic existentialism. Voegelin and Montgomery, like Cheney, often seem to lump all branches of existentialism together. Thus Montgomery wrote: "There is a quality common in discourses out of this new Promethean assault upon being called Existentialism . . . a quality which signals the 'nonphilosophical intention.' " Montgomery, at the same time, quoted Voegelin's incorrect definition of at least religious existentialism: "Existentialism 'ironically takes its name from the denial of existence to everything but the moment of man's flight from existence toward an eschatological future.' "[20]

Marcel himself, in describing Picard and his philosophy, noted that his method is like Nietzsche's, a method most simply defined by Jerome Taylor in discussing Walker Percy's existential viewpoint: "Existentialism is the rather broad movement of thought, ranging from atheistic to Christian, that insists that the important concern is the existing person as

---

[19]Gabriel Marcel, Introduction, *The Flight From God,* iii.
[20]Marion Montgomery, *Why Flannery O'Connor Stayed at Home,* 205.

over against any speculative intellectual system."[21] Walter Kaufmann, a leading authority on the subject, defines existentialism as a label for several widely different revolts against traditional philosophy, whose one essential feature is "their perfervid individualism."[22] Montgomery rightly emphasized the role of Aquinas and Voegelin in O'Connor's thought but not a single reference to Buber, Picard, or Guardini exists in his lengthy philosophical work on O'Connor. For this reason, in spite of his excellent understanding of O'Connor the insider who could accommodate herself to systems and hierarchies, Montgomery did not dig deeply enough into her apocalyptic Catholicism. Percy, for instance, is only mentioned three times by Montgomery, and Marcel gets only four references. Marcel, in particular, put his primary emphasis on love and intuition. In fact, Marcel said of Picard the man that "With him intuition is everything," that he was "spontaneity and life itself," that he was a "religious man" who was "always in communication with simple people, real people" and that he had a "horror of pretentiousness." If I were to describe O'Connor the person as I knew her, I would say that the above statements all would apply to her, except that she was not "all" intuition. She was as a writer, a thinker, and a person often intuitive, but she was also orderly and systematic in her thinking. Nevertheless, it is clear from both her fiction and her essays that she thought about religion and life generally from the standpoint not of systems of thought but from the viewpoint of the individual's search for a better way of life than the one she found everywhere around her as she was growing up in a Southern environment that seemed to block the individual's search for a meaningful existence.

That the individual—and the rebellious individual at that—is at the center of her work can be seen in reading *Wise Blood, The Violent Bear It Away*, and most of her short stories. In 1962, O'Connor made it clear to Granville Hicks that the religious individual was central to her work: " 'I'm not interested in the sects or sects: I'm concerned with the religious individual, the backwoods prophet.' "[23] She linked religion and the backwoods prophet because, for her, religion in the city was primarily a middle-class kind of "insurance," which is what she thought most

---

[21]Jerome Taylor, *In Search of Self* (Cambridge MA: Cowley Publications, 1986) 1.

[22]Walter Kaufmann, *Existentialism from Dostoevsky to Sartre* (New York: Meridian Books, 1956) 11.

[23]Granville Hicks, "A Writer at Home with her Heritage," *Saturday Review* (12 May 1962): 22.

American Catholics and Protestants sought in their religious practice. And even when, like Hazel Motes, the backwoods prophet is in revolt against Christ, something within him draws him back to authentic faith. He is, as she has said, a Christian in spite of himself. I began with Hicks's article in my own study of O'Connor from the viewpoint of religious existentialism, an article entitled "Flannery O'Connor: Georgia's Theological Storyteller." She read it in manuscript and approved of it except for one small point. I accepted her suggestion for a change and later she wrote to Louise Abbot about the article: "He sent me a paper on my stuff which he read recently at Georgia State. I liked it very much, much more than the last one" (*HB*, 567). My emphasis on her thought being similar to that of the religious existentialists was very strong in this paper, and she obviously agreed with my viewpoint.

As I pointed out in two articles of mine that she read and approved of, O'Connor's chief emphasis in her existential fiction is on the individual who is destructive for the very sake of destruction, that criminal for whom evil is its own reward.[24] She told me in 1958 that the best letters she received about her work were from prisoners in penitentiaries, and these letters helped to make her knowledge of the destructive criminal's inner nature accurate. The fact that Milledgeville itself was the site of the state penitentiary until it was moved to Reidsville in 1938 as well as the fact that Milledgeville has always been the home of the state insane asylum (to be sent to "Milledgeville" is a term every Georgian has often heard) undoubtedly had much to do with O'Connor's awareness of violence and human destructiveness. But in writing about O'Connor's awareness of destructiveness, I have always emphasized her continual linking of individual destructiveness to an involvement of Satan in human affairs. O'Connor's view of Satan, it must always be emphasized, is in keeping with orthodox Catholic theology. In dealing with what I have called the insider aspects of O'Connor's conscious thought, for instance, Montgomery has been excellent, stating clearly and often that position as being "based on Saint Thomas, as she affirms."[25] Thus Montgomery spoke of O'Connor as a "reactionary and dogmatic witness to the trans-

---

[24]See my articles, "Flannery O'Connor's View of God and Man," *Studies in Short Fiction* 1 (Spring 1964): 200-206, and "Flannery O'Connor: Georgia's Theological Storyteller," in *The Humanities in the Contemporary South* (Atlanta: Georgia State College, 1968).

[25]Montgomery, *Why Flannery O'Connor Stayed at Home*, 236.

cendent" and, quoting the author's best-known statement about Satan, pointed out her belief that "we need . . . 'a sense of evil which sees the devil as a real spirit who must be made to name himself with his specific personality for every occasion.' "[26]

Montgomery as a critic who documented in great detail the orthodox thought of O'Connor is hard to disagree with. And yet, when we look at her work, we see that strong Jansenist outlook that Allen Tate and her friend John Hawkes, among others, called attention to. We see characters continually caught up in an evil they can neither understand nor escape and who can hardly name Satan as the enemy because they are only vaguely aware, if at all, of the diabolical presence. O'Connor, for instance, never wrote in her fiction about a Catholic priest who as exorcist names Satan and communicates with him and finally drives him out of a house, a town, or a person. Such events have been common enough in popular Gothic fiction and drama. The reasons that she did not are two: she had no experience with Catholic or any other kinds of exorcism, in spite of her reading in Aquinas and Augustine, and she drew much of her inspiration from writers like West, Mauriac, and Bernanos who reveal in their fiction a far stronger sense of evil than they do of good.

O'Connor herself made clear in her best essay, "Some Aspects of the Grotesque in Southern Fiction," that the "writer's initially set going by literature more than by life," and she might well have added more than by abstract thought. Thus, in reading Mauriac and Bernanos, she found a fictional world in which evil generally seemed to triumph over good. She had found the same kind of world presented in the work of her earliest inspirers to writing fiction—Poe and Hawthorne. These writers, and Hawthorne in particular, helped her to see that what she was writing was not so much realistic fiction as what Hawthorne called the romance. In speaking of the "modern romance tradition" in "Some Aspects of the Grotesque in Southern Fiction," she made it clear that, though these works of romance will be misunderstood, they will possess a "vitality" all of their own. O'Connor's romances have proved to have a vitality for many readers, but some of these readers find her emphasis on evil too great for a full acceptance of her work—whereas others, aware of her old-fashioned Catholic orthodoxy, see her as the shining hope for the development of an American religious fiction, which she might indeed be

---

[26]Ibid., 77.

but not necessarily because her consciously held theology was orthodox. Yet much of O'Connor's vitality comes from what Joseph K. Davis has called her fictional "formulations" which, "if often quite beautiful in their artistic executions, are terrifying and ugly in their revelations of the awful powers of the demonic in human life."[27]

Certainly the most extensive and searching article to this date on the problem of evil in Faulkner and O'Connor, Davis's "Time and the Demonic in William Faulkner and Flannery O'Connor," reveals how these two great modern Southern authors draw heavily from both the literature and history of a turbulent and—due to slavery and defeat in war—a deeply wounded South in order to record both human and social devastation. Thus, for Davis, "O'Connor's fictions, thoroughly grounded within a theological point of view, reveal the terrible chaos of the contemporary world and the gathering storms of intensifying demonic activities."[28]

O'Connor underlined in her reading of Mauriac's *Memoires Interieures* the following passage:

> Here I touch on what, to my mind, gives so great value to *The Scarlet Letter*. This book furnishes us a key to what seems the most impenetrable of all mysteries, especially to the believer: the mystery of evil. Evil is in the world, and in ourselves. Yet, "all is Grace." Those are the last words of Bernanos's country priest.[29]

These lines by Mauriac, incorporating his thought and referring to the work of Hawthorne and Bernanos, two of O'Connor's greatest intertexts, sum up O'Connor's desire to depict grace as well as demonism in her fiction. On a few occasions the action of grace does appear, but the demonic is far stronger, I believe, in her work than she even knew, certainly more than she intended. And one may well ask why. I have already mentioned intertextual connections and would add that, although the lines quoted above from Mauriac's memoir state his recognition of grace and evil as existing side by side, there still is in the best work of Mauriac that sense of an all-pervading evil which dominates modern life. Jean-Paul

---

[27]Joseph K. Davis, "Time and the Demonic in William Faulkner and Flannery O'Connor," *Studies in the Literary Imagination* 20 (Fall 1987): 143.

[28]Ibid.

[29]Arthur F. Kinney, *Flannery O'Connor's Library: Resources of Being* (Athens: University of Georgia Press, 1985) 132.

Sartre's article "Mauriac and Freedom," published as early as 1939 and vigorously attacked by Mauriac, makes the point, in the words of Harry T. Moore, that all of the French Catholic's characters are "victims of original sin, have no freedom to develop but are hopelessly doomed."[30] Similarly, Bernanos, whose novels sometimes include Satan as a character, revealed in his work, according to Moore, a Christianity that is "always essentially ferocious."[31]

Particularly in *The Violent Bear It Away*, O'Connor's major novel, which contains Satan as a character and two Protestants continually tempted by him, there is a quality that can only be called ferocious. For many readers, this book that she saw as her greatest literary accomplishment—and I think I agree with her—in places seems repulsive in the ferocity of its characters and the terror associated with the power of evil. Yet the book, as Harold Bloom and Stanley Edgar Hyman have maintained, is essentially in the line of Mark Twain's *Huckleberry Finn*. O'Connor drew something very profound out of modern Southern life that was also present in the region in earlier centuries. And we may say that since Twain is as fully American as he is Southern, she has extended one American literary vision—the power of evil to crush good. Not only in the well-known gloominess of Poe, and later Twain, Faulkner, Williams, Warren, or Styron, but in most of the literature of modern naturalism in the North or West there is a strong sense of evil triumphant. Considering that we find just as much gloom in French literature from Flaubert and Baudelaire to the present, we cannot blame the pessimism of America's serious writers on the failure of civilization in the New World or on the evils of slavery and the plantation system, though these factors are no doubt significant. More than anything else, I think, the defeat of the vast utopian dreams created by the French Revolution led to what Sir Kenneth Clark in his *Civilisation* called the age following the revolution one of the "fallacies of hope." A study of the South after the American Revolution and before the beginning of the Cotton Kingdom after 1810 reveals a region under the spell of utopian dreams voiced by Jefferson and others who believed that French revolutionary ideals would eventually triumph. Of this "Gallomania" in the South after the American Revolution, Page Smith wrote:

---

[30]Harry T. Moore, *Twentieth-Century French Literature* (New York: Dell Publishing Co., 1966) 105.
[31]Ibid.

Moreover, Gallomania was not to be a passing fancy. It rapidly became one of the determining factors in American politics. Every political figure must take its stand and be measured on the French question. While the divisions were roughly class divisions in the Northern and Middle states, they became largely sectional in the South where yeoman farmers and plantation owners alike cast their lot with the French cause.[32]

Milledgeville became the Georgia capital in 1807, and there is still about it in the twentieth century an aura of those early idealistic days of the republic. Although most of the town's antebellum homes are in the Greek revival style, homes thereby associated with the Cotton Kingdom, O'Connor and her mother regularly ate lunch at the Sanford House, an example of Federalist architecture dating from 1820 and recalling a time before the fanaticism of cotton barons defending slavery and states' rights.

Various reasons account for O'Connor's dislike of all forms of utopian thinking. Joyce Carol Oates wrote in her analysis of O'Connor's apocalyptic view that the Georgia author was caught up in Dostoevski's "reactionary" views. O'Connor was deeply read in Dostoevski, but, though she admired his religious vision, she never tried to write like him. Much closer to O'Connor's way of thinking was the perennial Catholic aversion to all utopian thinking because it suggested a social organization at variance with the Church's belief in the Augustinian City of God. Also, as one who had a medieval mind that took Dante and Aquinas to be its natural intellectual food, O'Connor saw utopian thinking, with all its secularism, as ignoring a view of life in which heaven, hell, and purgatory are central concepts. In one letter O'Connor stated quite simply and seriously that she awaited purgatory. She also absorbed some of the thinking of the most widely read American theologian of the period from 1945 to 1960, Reinhold Niebuhr, whose work marked a return to the concept of sin, discarded by liberal theologians, and to a belief in the impossibility of shaping history, with all of its ambiguities, into any kind of political or social perfection. With the end of World War II and the soon-to-be Cold War, the old idealism of an earlier period was rapidly declining. There is no sign that O'Connor ever went through a period of utopian beliefs, as many youths have done. Having early read Poe and Hawthorne and later Conrad, she always seemed to have a tough-minded

---

[32]Page Smith, *The Shaping of America*, 3 vols. (New York: McGraw-Hill Book Co., 1966) 3:105.

view of human imperfection, which her strict Catholic upbringing always supported.

Utopianism is an important concept for considering O'Connor's intellectual view because its continuing presence for her was a sign that most of the world's population was caught up in a secular view that had behind it a kind of deism, the belief that God, if he existed, could not or would not interfere with the world. The central fact of modern life in her worldview was that this way of thinking had led to a belief that "God is dead" and the result of this, for her medieval mind, was the triumph of Satan in the world, largely unrecognized, but an active spirit, not principle, which was destroying the world. A modern Jesuit whose work O'Connor knew, Leon Christiani, in his *Evidence of Satan in the Modern World*, stated quite clearly her viewpoint: "For a Catholic, Satan is *Someone*. Satan is not an abstraction, an invention, a character in fiction, the hero of a novel."[33] Like Christiani, she believed that part of the Church's work was to warn always of Satan's activity. But, as one with an apocalyptic imagination, O'Connor had at the center of her thought a prototype of a prophet whose continuing task was to point out that only through grace received by faith (the particular religious emphasis of religious existentialists from Kierkegaard to the present) could the world push Lucifer off center stage so that religion could be what it was in the Middle Ages, the central activity of humanity. All of the above she talked to me about at length on various occasions and her letters are full of these ideas. They are at the center of her thinking. They are also related to her considerable skills as a literary critic, which we need now to examine.

In arguing that O'Connor had a well-developed intellectual worldview, I would suggest that she answered for herself Kant's four philosophical questions: what can we know? (what the Holy Spirit tells us), what can we hope? (to enter heaven), what should we do? (follow God's teaching), and what are we? (children of God). She also had a philosophy of history that could be summed up in the words of the American novelist whose thought was most like hers, Walker Percy. For Percy, the modern age began around three centuries ago and "has already ended." It will probably be known as "the Secular Era, which came to an end

---

[33]Leon Christiani, *Evidence of Satan in the Modern World* (New York: Aaron Books, 1961) 186.

with the catastrophes of the twentieth century."[34] Percy was more of a Christian humanist than O'Connor was, and I think his essays and novels reveal that her answer to Kant's question, "What is man?," was much narrower than the more experienced Percy's answer. Had she lived longer, I believe she would have gained a deeper and wider knowledge of the human soul and human society. But she is far stronger than Percy in the realm of imagination and sheer poetic power of language. Whether she took her own apocalyptic forecasts of human catastrophe in her novels with total seriousness, I cannot say. She did not entirely believe, with Percy, in "a discredited Christendom."[35] She believed most people *thought* Christendom was discredited, but her hope was—and she was forecasting this in her fiction—that prophets might once again make Christianity credible. Her fiction is in part about the end of one world and the hopeful beginning of another. How much actual catastrophe in worldly terms there would be was, for her, yet to be seen. But the tangible catastrophe was the progress of Satan in the modern world. It might be that eventually she would have agreed with Percy about total catastrophe, as expressed when he wrote the following:

> So too may it be useful to write a novel about the end of the world. Perhaps it is only through the conjuring up of catastrophe, the destruction of all Exxon signs, and the sprouting of vines in the church pews, that the novelist can make vicarious use of catastrophe in order that he and his reader may come to themselves.[36]

---

[34]Walker Percy, *The Message in the Bottle*, 114.
[35]Ibid., 118.
[36]Ibid.

Chapter 4

The Emerging Woman of Letters

By 1960 it had become clear from both public addresses and from her published occasional prose that Flannery O'Connor was becoming, like her mentor Caroline Gordon, a woman of letters. Her personal correspondence indicates that she was far more than a professional writer or even one seeking to establish herself among the nation's "serious writers." She had, since even the late forties, been deeply immersed in the life of literature and everything related to it. Soon after arriving in New York, she had found the Fitzgeralds, a couple intensively devoted to literature, and then in 1951 she began to work with Caroline Gordon, who, with her husband Allen Tate, was devoted to literature in a way that only a woman of letters could be—which is to say that she was concerned with literature in all its aspects, with literary criticism as well as with belles lettres, with philosophy and theology as they related to literature, as well as with the actual people and events of the past and present that provided the raw material for fiction. Without Gordon and the Fitzgeralds, O'Connor might not have emerged as a woman of letters. Since the life of letters must involve a great deal of interaction between writers, these three people were very important in helping O'Connor in what for her, even in her college life, was a profound devotion to literature.

Gore Vidal, in a 1988 radio interview, said that the only writer in America he knew who did not talk exclusively with other writers about advances and royalties was Saul Bellow, but one could have said the same thing of Walker Percy. And, in her lifetime as an emerging woman of letters, one certainly would have to say O'Connor was a writer who almost never talked of monetary success, fame, or notoriety. Along with a small amount of gossip, her main subject of conversation with anyone really interested in literature past, present, or future was the life of letters. In spite of this fact, O'Connor is still not generally seen as a woman of letters but as a kind of recluse with a morbid interest in the sort of grotesque characters the South has been noted for in its fiction. The fault is partly that of the press. When *The Violent Bear It Away* appeared, *Time* magazine in its review suggested that the author was doing not much more than poking fun at her Southern grotesques. And after her death, when O'Connor had become established as a significant American writer, *Time* printed a two-page essay on her life and work that made her life appear to be that of a recluse on a Georgia farm, at best a kind of twentieth-century Emily Dickinson.

Possibly, the prejudice against her true vocation exhibited not only by much of the press but even by some intellectuals and academics sprang from O'Connor's origins in the small-town South. That a woman from Milledgeville could in her early years decide she would become a significant American writer, then set about her task by attending an outstanding school of creative writing, impressing its director and, with his help, getting published, and then go on to New York and in her early twenties have a novel published that would become a classic, has seemed improbable to many. The chief reason is not that she was from the South, but that she was a woman. Truman Capote in Monroeville, Alabama, would have the same kind of ideas, would go to New York to be publish- ed early, and would soon become established as a cosmopolitan, success- ful "serious" writer. It should be easy to understand why Gordon and O'Connor both had mixed feelings about Capote, even some feelings of envy, because they too had apprenticed themselves early to literature, had gone to New York to seek success, and had achieved some recognition. And yet neither writer was fully accepted on her own terms. A friend of Gordon's and O'Connor's, Katherine Anne Porter, would also not find that large acceptance Capote early achieved until 1962 with the publica- tion of *Ship of Fools*. By then, a new feminism was beginning to appear. This same feminism would help Welty by 1970 move from minor literary status to the major status she deserved.

Carson McCullers is, of course, one exception in the struggle for literary recognition by a serious writer who was also female. But it is possible that her heavy drinking, her marital problems, her continuing illness, and her failure somehow to write very much in that new literary period beginning after 1945 helped to disarm the threat she posed to a male, largely unconsciously chauvinistic literary establishment. But also McCullers was not an intellectual. This fact would later help Porter and Welty with many members of the national literary establishment. To anyone who knew her or her occasional prose, O'Connor clearly was an intellectual like Bellow or Percy in that her literary intellectualism was in the continental mold. She had early read, understood, and digested French and German thinkers and made use of their work in both her fiction and nonfiction. As I have sought to suggest, her intellectual viewpoint was totally interrelated to her deep immersion in the writing of a variety of literary masters. O'Connor's head and heart were never separated; she read with both her mind and emotions, and her comments on books in her letters indicate this fact. She generally read both to understand and to experience totally, and she hoped her own writing would be thus approached by readers. In Britain, giants like George Eliot or Virginia Woolf, or lesser writers like Muriel Spark or Iris Murdoch, have been accepted as both thinkers and artists who could capture segments of existence in their evolved literary visions, but, in America before 1960, women writers could only be accepted for offering an insight into social manners, like Edith Wharton or Ellen Glasgow, or into some corner of American decadence—Welty, Cather, and McCullers, for instance. But any American writer who was a woman could hardly be accepted as a major figure in fiction because it was thought that women had little to say in fiction that was profound. The popular press has clamored throughout the century for a Great American Novel, but only men are supposed to be able to write it. The general ignoring of Cather's greatest work, until recently, is an example of this prejudice.

Caroline Gordon and Katherine Anne Porter had struggled for years to be recognized as serious writers and even as women of letters along European lines, but it would be Flannery O'Connor, more than any other American woman of her time, who would, as she neared death in 1964, begin to achieve recognition as an emerging woman of letters. The recognition came because of the seriousness of her devotion to her art, the weight of her intellect, which was manifested in readings and lectures at significant universities like Vanderbilt, Notre Dame, and Emory, and, finally, because of her recognition as a major writer by prominent literary figures like John Crowe Ransom, Robert Penn Warren, Randall Jarrell, Robert Lowell, and Elizabeth Bishop. Beyond these reasons, there was in her speeches, her occasional prose, and her meaningful comments already being circulated in print an awareness of the depths of modern literature found only in significant literary figures. Above all else, there was in O'Connor a budding literary critic at once both intuitive and knowledgeable, a critic that would have continued to emerge to the extent that O'Connor as novelist, critic, and woman of letters might well have attained the status of an American Virginia Woolf.

O'Connor's powerful intellect and her profound intuition were clear from the very beginning of our conversations. Many of these conversations, as I have indicated, were devoted to discussions of literature, theology, and religion. The intuitive aspects of her critical mind appeared early in her largely evaluative criticism, consisting of prophecies about future careers of several figures new to American letters. One was James Dickey, whom she mentioned in our first conversation, in August 1958, as the important new poet in the South. Since Dickey in 1958 had not published a volume of poems, it sounded to me at the time that her judgement, which was quite soberly delivered, was somewhat premature. In an 11 March 1958 letter, one of her two references to Dickey in letters to others is as follows: "Last Sunday I was visited by a poet named James Dickey who is an admirer of Robert [Lowell]" (*HB*, 272). In a 27 July 1958 letter to John Hawkes, she wrote simply, "I have a friend, James Dickey, a poet, who was down here recently to show his little boy the ponies. I told him I was reading your books and it turned out he had read all of them" (*HB*, 292). Less than a month later, she assured me of Dickey's great significance as a Southern poet, and this judgement turned out to be correct, though Dickey at this time was receiving no great attention. Dickey also in 1958 was aware of her presence as a serious woman of letters. He told me in conversation in 1986 that, when he began to write, she was the only writer in Georgia who "was doing anything."

Also in 1958, O'Connor told me of a new writer that she believed would go far, John Updike. In September 1963, she wrote in a letter to Cecil Dawkins that she was disappointed with *Rabbit Run*: "I liked Updike's first novel, *The Poorhouse Fair*, but that *Rabbit Run* thing you can have and the other I didn't attempt" (*HB*, 540). In an earlier letter, she said of *Rabbit Run* that the "sex in it is laid on too heavy" (*HB*, 420). But her feeling—and it was largely an intuitive feeling she had—that Updike in *The Poorhouse Fair* was essentially a religious writer, one much like herself, would later be borne out by his religious fiction of the seventies and eighties. As a lover of Hawthorne, I think that she would have approved particularly of *Roger's Version* and *S*. O'Connor's attitude toward the reading of new fiction can be seen at the end of the Dawkins's letter, in which she discussed Updike. "Everybody tells me," she wrote, "to read *Catch-22*, and I will when I find it in paperback. No bookstore here but I am going to Atlanta tomorrow" (*HB*, 540). The variety of her reading and her enthusiasm for an author she loved can be seen in the next sentences of the same letter: "Right now I'm reading *Eichmann in Jerusalem*. My what a book. I admire that old lady extremely" (*HB*, 540). O'Connor's profound awareness of the Holocaust is made clear in a letter mentioning "that old lady," Hannah Arendt, two days earlier: "I've always been haunted by the boxcars, but they were actually the least of it. And old Hannah is as sharp as they come" (*HB*, 539). The boxcars of the Holocaust appeared as an image in "Revelation," possible the most powerful work of her second collection of stories.

The great admiration O'Connor had for the intellect of Hannah Arendt is paralleled by her admiration for the intellects of other powerful women, among them, Simone Weil and Caroline Gordon. In discussing the critical mind of O'Connor, it is always necessary to remember the part that Gordon as mentor played in the development of the younger woman's mind. I could never perceive that O'Connor was ever really in awe of anyone, including Gordon, because she had too much self-possession to engage in any form of hero worship, although she seemed at times in discussing Robert Lowell to be slightly awed by his poetic powers. I attended a conference at Vanderbilt in 1959 when she did seem briefly in awe of Robert Penn Warren, but I do not believe anyone that she admired even as much as she did Warren or Gordon could ever overcome her mind enough to make her accept a literary judgment she did not firmly believe in. This should be kept in mind in assessing what I believe to be the single most important literary influence in her work, that of James Joyce. O'Connor did not passively receive literary influences from other writers, but, especially in the case of major influences like those of Bernanos, Mauriac, and Joyce, she made mature critical judgments even as she intuitively and intellectually took into herself what she needed from the writers she most admired. Her excellent critical judgment and her use of writers she admired to inspire her own work are major aspects of her role as a woman of letters.

I have already discussed how much Bernanos and Mauriac meant to O'Connor in terms of both literary and intellectual influence. But O'Connor herself makes clear that James Joyce meant more to her than any other writer. It was the mark of O'Connor's mind, one that was both intuitively and intellectually attuned to literary criticism, that she could read Joyce and go right to the heart of what she needed from this master of modern literature. In a letter to Father John McCown, she contrasted the influence of the French Catholic novelists who meant so much to her and the influence of Hemingway and Joyce on her work:

> I have read almost everything that Bloy, Bernanos, and Mauriac have written. The Catholic fiction writers have very little highpowered "Catholic" fiction to influence them except that written by these three and Greene. But at the some point reading them reaches the place of diminishing returns and you get more benefit reading someone like Hemingway, where there is apparently a hunger for a Catholic completeness in life, or Joyce who can't get rid of it no matter what he does. It may be a matter of recognizing the Holy Ghost in fiction by the way he chooses to conceal himself (*HB*, 130).

In this concise statement O'Connor revealed her continuing awareness that good writing springs not only from the author's relationship with life but also from her intertextual connections with other authors. Hemingway and Joyce possessed qualities of vision and expression that O'Connor deeply needed, and she readily turned to them for inspiration.

Many critics have rightly noted that O'Connor as a critic expressed herself with a trenchancy and depth of understanding seldom found in the lectures and essays of *Mystery and Manners.* An O'Connor that was more relaxed than the one who was writing formal essays or speeches, tasks which as a "repressed teacher" (her term for herself) she took very seriously, could in letters and conversations go straight to the core of literary matters. Her reason for needing Hemingway is apparent, because of his precision of statement and his poetic qualities. She rightly knew she could not compete with Faulkner, Wolfe, or other Southern writers like Warren or Welty on their terms. What she brought to Southern fiction that was new was what Hemingway at his best had—a bright and simple poetic imagery that would stay for years in the minds of readers. O'Connor's friend Elizabeth Bishop, a poet seeking a simple but powerful imagery, recognized this fact about her work:

> I am sure her few books will live on and on in American literature. They are narrow, possibly, but they are clear, hard, vivid and full of bits of description, phrases, and odd insights that contains more real poetry than a dozen books of poems (*CS*, xvi).

Yet her turning to Hemingway for an intertextual relationship leading to a diamond-hard poetic prose was not as simple a matter as it might appear because for literary inspiration she had also earlier turned to Faulkner and West. Not long after O'Connor met Robert Fitzgerald in 1949, she urged him to read both authors. "I owe to Flannery my first reading of *Miss Lonelylights* that winter," Fitzgerald wrote, "as I owe my reading of *As I Lay Dying*" (*ERMC*, xv). At this time, while still writing *Wise Blood*, she was under the influence of West's simple style and his use of the absurd. In Faulkner's *As I Lay Dying*, she also found a sense of the absurd and a deep concern for simple country folk of the kind she herself sought to portray in *Wise Blood*. Yet, as she continued her reading in Faulkner, as she in fact told me, she found in his work a kind of complexity of style and organization that was alien to her, even though she admired his imaginative power. This statement validates Harold Bloom's concept of the anxiety of influence—the fear of authors that they will be held back in their literary efforts to find their own style by the styles of admired precursors. O'Connor thus wrote to "A" in 1958: "I keep clear of Faulkner so that my own little boat won't get swamped" (*HB*, 273).

If Faulkner is rejected as an admired precursor by O'Connor, one may ask why would she not have rejected a writer like Joyce, who is possibly even more complex than Faulkner? The reason is that Joyce's work contained something O'Connor very much needed. What it was, Walker Percy told us, was the power of the dark regions of the soul. Percy too needed that element of Joyce and rightly he linked O'Connor to it. The old vocabulary of Christianity is worn out, Percy told us in "A Novel About the End of the World." Like Joyce's Dedalus, the new religious novelist (and Percy mentioned O'Connor in the same paragraphs as one of these) "calls on every ounce of cunning, craft, and guile he can muster from the darker regions of his soul" to write a new kind of religious novel.[1] It would be a kind of fiction beyond any found in Bernanos or Mauriac, even though for O'Connor this fiction would include some of what they also had accomplished.

O'Connor's deep involvement with Joyce is related first to her chief theme: the individual who cannot free himself from Jesus no matter how often or in how many ways he attempts to flee God. But, secondly, it is also related to her profound concern with art in all its manifestations. O'Connor was born a Roman Catholic and always remained one, but she was in many ways also a convert to the life of the artist. And more than anyone else, her mentor Caroline Gordon was deeply involved in this conversion. Waldron, pointing to Gordon's key critical concepts as expressed in *How to Read a Novel*, wrote: "The book distills a great many

---

[1]Walker Percy, *The Message in the Bottle* (New York: Farrar, Straus, and Giroux, 1979) 118.

of Caroline's ideas about the novel, and pays tribute to Flaubert, James, and Joyce, her second Holy Trinity."[2] Undoubtedly, Gordon as mentor helped to lead O'Connor in the direction of master literary artists like Flaubert, James, and Joyce, but O'Connor had that kind of stubborn literary-critical mind that made her verify her own intertextual relationships. Thus she plunged on her own into the literary works of Joyce and others to find and use what she needed. She had worked as a writer too long and too hard on her own before encountering her literary mentor to follow blindly even so profound a critical intelligence as Gordon's. Yet these two women had a way of becoming deeply involved in similar writers. Thus, for both of them, Joyce was not only a great literary artist but also profoundly Christian. For a lecture at the College of St. Thomas on the Catholic revival in literature, Waldron reported that "Caroline read and reread Catholic writers and gamely set out to prove her latest thesis, for which she credited Maritain: that Joyce and Flaubert were more Christian writers than Mauriac because they were better writers."[3] What Joyce above all else gave Gordon and O'Connor was the Catholic emphasis on the role of the feminine principle in both literature and life.

With the subject of O'Connor's approach to the feminine we are at the center of O'Connor's role as insider-outsider. As insider she followed the powerful masculine attitudes of the Southern hierarchy, which in many areas after the Civil War fell under the control of women. These attitudes were based, for Southern Catholics and Protestants, on the painful need to establish a new hierarchical control—this time in conjunction with Northern capital. As elsewhere in the Western world, the desire for hierarchical power meant puritanism in its many forms, which in turn meant a repression of the feminine principle in general and of the sexual principle in particular. In the young O'Connor, who was seeking, successfully as it turned out, to establish herself as a published writer on New York terms, one taken seriously by cosmopolitan critics, we see the employment of her insider talents for hard work, for repression, and for getting along with influential Northerners who could help her. The young O'Connor early revealed a talent for achieving literary success, at least among serious authors. As a woman who took her own femininity quite seriously and as a traditional Catholic who, like all her Irish forebears, took the Virgin Mary very seriously indeed, she dedicated herself, in a

---

[2]Ann Waldron, *Close Connections* (New York: G. P. Putman's Sons, 1987) 344.
[3]Ibid., 297.

way that Joyce did, to exploring the role of the feminine in life. In order to exalt the feminine in an age where masculinity seemed dominant everywhere, both Joyce and O'Connor sought a path of exile. As the greatest exile in English-speaking literature of the century, Joyce represented to O'Connor a writer who had the courage to go to great cities like Paris to escape a much beloved homeland whose inhabitants always tried to repress his deepest literary powers, which sprang from a feminine vision and from a poetry celebrating that feminine principle embodied in his greatest character, Molly Bloom. The same could also be said of D. H. Lawrence or E. M. Forster, both seeking to discover thereupon a repressed sexuality, or of Henry Adams, Henry James, or T. S. Eliot, who sought and found their own visions of the feminine in several European cultures.

Robert Fitzgerald was correct in assessing O'Connor's acceptance of exile when he wrote that "Flannery was out to be a writer on her own and had no plans to go back to live in Georgia" (*ERMC*, xiv). When the Fitzgeralds discovered O'Connor in New York, they found a dedicated writer who had accepted exile but one also who had remained thoroughly Southern, just as Joyce in Paris remained thoroughly Irish. Yet, in Sally Fitzgerald's already quoted passage on O'Connor's return to the South to stay, after lupus had done its horrible work on her body, we see the determination of the writer to live with the South and even use it, as she often does in her letters, to beat Northerners over the head for the failures of their region. But while remaining outwardly hierarchical, O'Connor the artist turned in her work, with her own deeply feminine vision, to consider the plight of those who were often ignored or even despised by the hierarchy—most children, blacks, foreigners, poor yeoman farmers, and religionists who were serious about their beliefs. All of these were outsiders in modern hierarchical communities, and all were in some ways similar to O'Connor. Finally, like Joyce, she took into account the work of modern urbanization, the rise of the great cities.

For Joyce and O'Connor, the great cities like New York with their centers where a new modernist culture was coming into being were places necessary for personal and artistic development. O'Connor and Joyce were escapees from the provincial cities of Atlanta and Dublin, but at the same time all cities were becoming what Oswald Spengler has called world megalopolises, which kill intellect and devalue provincial energies. In my own article study of Joyce, O'Connor, and the megalopolis, I noted that for both Joyce and O'Connor the great symbol of alienation "was the megalopolian city, that urban sprawl which had been cut loose from the moorings of earlier centers of cultural development that once formed the basis for these cities."[4] Alienation, which causes that strange paralysis of spirit that Joyce found everywhere in Ireland and the world, was the chief theme of both O'Connor and Joyce until their final works—the later stories like "Revelation" and *Finnegans Wake*— when the two sought and found muted visions of an emerging world community. Critics caught up in O'Connor's brilliant rural scenes of blacks, Southern "aristocrats," yeoman farmers, and religious proletarians struggling in country life have failed to notice that the struggles are all related to a life fading rapidly to make way for an encroaching urbanism. And in spite of long years on a farm and her love of animals, O'Connor was always more urban in her literary vision than is generally realized. The central fact of her creative life—the vision itself—sprang from more than a Blakean cultivation; it came in part from long hours of rocking in the afternoons on the porch at Andalusia. It also required continuing conversation, study, and letter-writing; the work, that is, of an emerging woman of letters.

Following the paths offered by her literary sister relationship with "A," the mentorship of Gordon, the involved letters and conversations with those at a distance like the Fitzgeralds, and associations with those like Sessions, Abbot, and myself, with whom she talked at Andalusia, O'Connor did what Joyce, Henry James, and Conrad did: she concerned herself deeply with thinking, writing, and talking about literature. The speeches at colleges and the occasional prose of *Mystery and Manners* revealed this, but the letters, containing most of her best remarks about literature, show her critical mind at its best, a mind that was both rational and intuitive, one that went to the heart of meaning and value in the works of many writers. Her letters are the best of any American writer of the post-World War II age. They are possibly equalled by one modern American writer born in the South, Conrad Aiken, a writer whose value she did not appreciate (there are two slighting remarks about him in the letters.) The two were born in houses that are almost in sight of each other in downtown Savannah. I conversed at length and corresponded with both, and I found both could talk with muted passion for several hours at a time about writers and literature. Once, in 1968, I urged Aiken

---

[4]Ted R. Spivey, "Flannery O'Connor, James Joyce and the City," *Studies in the Literary Imagination* 20/2 (Fall 1987): 92.

to read O'Connor's work, and he pointed at a volume of her work on a shelf and said a friend had brought it. He suggested that she was too minor a writer for him to involve himself with. He was in his own eyes, and rightly, I think, a major American critic and man of letters. He was hardly aware, at seventy-eight, of the new kind of literary generation that O'Connor represented.

As people who had the life of Savannah firmly stamped upon their minds, Aiken and O'Connor had absorbed the urbanity of a small city that, when they were young there, still drew cultural power from London and Paris. But the two suffered wounds of the soul there, Aiken more than O'Connor. Aiken went to the source of his wounds, which grew out of the murder-suicide of his parents. After several attempts at suicide, Aiken would resolve the old conflicts. O'Connor's psychic wounds received in Savannah remained hidden, most of them even to her; had she dealt with these wounds, she might have understood herself better. Some of the wounds were possibly connected with her Irish descent. Once I told her I had been to Savannah and had tried to find Bonaventure Cemetery, where Aiken's parents were buried and where he later would rest. Instead, I had found Savannah's large Irish cemetery, and I walked through it noting the graves of many Flannerys and O'Connors. Then I described to her a Civil War statue I saw in the cemetery, one dedicated to all the Savannah Irish who had died for the South, and I spoke of the strange and sad beauty of the cemetery, a kind of beauty that certain places in Savannah and Charleston sometimes possess. She said nothing but turned her head away from me. On her face was a look of pain.

The deepest element in O'Connor, except for her religion and her love of the literary art, was her Irish heritage. And that heritage is connected with religion and literature because the Irish, whom the English so long had sought to disinherit, always had Ireland, Catholicism, and their own native folklore. O'Connor had felt it all in Joyce, including his flight, which was finally a failure, from Catholicism. And the Irish heritage gave O'Connor another arrow in her literary quiver, that of social critic in the visionary Blakean sense. She carried in her mind that holocaust of nineteenth-century potato famines (thus her admiration for Hannah Arendt) and the awareness that the American Irish were despised foreigners, even though they often became quickly involved in Southern society, some even becoming "aristocrats" who furnished soldiers for the Confederacy. But one wonders if the whole Irish-Southern aristocrat's life was not a kind of pose, hiding the powerful, never to be fully repressed, Irish suffering of centuries.

I believe O'Connor, had she lived, would have eventually begun to face the wounds of her Irish past and, through her writing, would have fruitfully exorcised these inherited traumas. O'Connor's Blakean social vision—the insights of a great social critic in letters—does in fact deal with the Irish past. Yet in all our American struggles to unearth black, Jewish, Hispanic suffering, and other agonies contained in our origins, we have not yet come to grips fully with Irish suffering. Once I glimpsed the depths of this suffering in the most learned and urbane man I ever met. A native New Yorker of Irish stock, the mythologist Joseph Campbell was telling me in 1963 that Aldous Huxley, whom he had never met, had come to New York and asked him to lunch. I asked Campbell what he thought of Huxley and he said he did not like him. I wondered why and he replied, "I don't like any Englishman." O'Connor never had that kind of inherited Irish prejudice, but the Irish roots in her were far more important than her readers usually realize. Yet the only really strong statement she ever made to me about the Irish was that they were mainly what was wrong with the Catholic Church in America and that she could say this because she was Irish. O'Connor thus did not have time, as she saw it, to deal consciously with problems of her Irish past because two other matters were sometimes fanatically, but, most often not, at the center of her thinking: religion and literature.

As a literary critic, O'Connor was capable of the kind of empiricism in artistic matters that is found in most modern formalist criticism. Inevitably, as a student of Caroline Gordon, she followed, at least some of the time, the paths of New Criticism. In helping Ben Griffith with a story he had sent her for her critical examination, O'Connor followed Gordon's (and James's) dictum that fiction must be presented in terms of felt experience. Of the action in Griffith's story, she wrote, "I mean you have to present it and leave it alone. You have to let the things in the story do the talking" (*HB*, 83). Then, to clinch her argument, she referred to the example of Joyce's "The Dead": "Do you know Joyce's story 'The Dead'? See how he makes the snow work in that story. Chekhov makes everything work—the air, the light, the cold, the diet, etc. Show these things and you don't have to say them" (*HB*, 84). As writer and woman of letters, O'Connor always revealed her fine sense of detail. As a writer who believed in the continuing process of rewriting, she seemed to be engaged in an endless quest for artistic perfection. And this quest was linked, as was the same quest in Gordon, to the instinct of a teacher of literature. Thus she ended her critique of Griffith's story by speaking of her pedagogical side: "If you do rewrite it, I hope you will let me see it again. This is just the repressed schoolteacher in me cropping out" (*HB*, 84).

By 1955, when she wrote the above critique, the New Criticism had reached its high-water mark, and decline in the movement could even then be detected. Beginning with archons of modernism like T. S. Eliot, Ezra Pound, and I. A. Richards and continuing with, among others, such major figures of Southern literature as John Crowe Ransom, Allen Tate, Robert Penn Warren, and Cleanth Brooks, the New Criticism from its beginnings was concerned with meaning as much as with form. But with the growing influence of Brooks and Warren's *Understanding Poetry*, the most significant of all college texts based on the New Criticism, there would be the inevitable emphasis on form to the exclusion of meaning. Interpretations and technical analysis would, with the aid of formulas, inevitably become facile and finally, in the hands of students and critics, often abused. O'Connor herself, in letters after 1955, would often take to task teachers and critics whose interpretations of symbolism in her own stories were heavy-handed. In her various attacks on simplistic formalism, O'Connor revealed her own distrust of separating in criticism problems of form from problems of meaning. And, for her, the problem of meaning was essentially a religious problem. In her conscious mind, O'Connor would never separate her profound concern for literary artistry from her Catholic beliefs.

The problem of symbolism was, for O'Connor, essential, and, in her most famous remark on the subject made to the renegade Catholic Mary McCarthy, she summed up her most basic belief concerning art and religion. McCarthy had said, as O'Connor related the matter in a letter to "A," that she thought of the Holy Ghost "as a symbol": "I then said, in a very shaky voice, 'Well if it's a symbol, to hell with it!' That was all the defense I was capable of but I realize now that this is all I will ever to able to say about it, outside of a story, except that it is the center of existence for me; all the rest of life is expendable" (*HB*, 125). For O'Connor, the *symbol*, as McCarthy used the term, is simply a pointer to something that is non-existent. But the true symbol in literature or religion was for O'Connor a sacrament, one that actually has the power to relate the individual to divine grace. Thus, without knowing it at the time, she was agreeing with Thomas Merton's insight in his article

"Symbolism: Communication or Communion?": "A true symbol takes us to the center of the circle, not to another point on the circumference. It is by symbolism that man enters affectively and consciously into contact with his own deepest self, with other men, and with God."[5]

O'Connor's awareness of the power contained in the affective symbol led her to think in terms of Joycean epiphany, and her profoundest stories culminate in epiphanic moments in which certain characters experience moments of grace or vision in which, as Merton put it, contact is made, no matter how briefly, with one's "own self, with other men [and women], and with God." As an emerging woman of letters who was increasingly concerned with literary criticism, O'Connor would, I believe, have moved more deeply into the meaning of the Joycean epiphany in both her work and that of writers of her own time. But her concern with vision, her own and others, would have led her beyond the Joycean epiphany to the kind of visionary experience found in her greatest single work, *The Violent Bear It Away*. This work is basic for understanding what Gordon called her "Blakean vision," but O'Connor was not given the time to find the meaning of the "Blakean" power which she above all others of her generation possessed. It is a power linked to what John Hawkes has called a "diabolical" force. The writer's imagination and the problems of the diabolical element both in artistic creation and in life itself were of great interest to her. Had she lived longer, she undoubtedly would have continued to explore various aspects of the diabolical, possibly much in the manner in which her favorite American Catholic novelist, J. F. Powers, had plunged into this element in his stories and in his novel *Morte D'Urban*, which she strongly urged me to read. To understand something of the complexity of this view of diabolism, I believe it will be necessary in the future to study O'Connor in greater depth as her work relates to both Joyce and Dante.

In her last years O'Connor was, in her related roles of critic and woman of letters, always seeking to understand the contemporary literary scene, but she was, in the development of her critical intellect, also trying to understand her own work. She was clearly not in the line of those modernist American authors like Faulkner and Hemingway who shrank from examining their own work critically and who ignored the critical and scholarly efforts of others who studied their work. O'Connor was, in

---

[5]Merton as quoted in Joseph Campbell's *Myths to Live By* (New York: Viking Press, 1972) 256-57.

her words, a "repressed schoolteacher," and she was also, without apology, a critic and an intellectual. She was, like Joyce and most other writers, careful not to become overly analytical in relation to her own work for fear, no doubt, that she might somehow harm her own creative power. For this reason she might well have been right to take with a grain of salt my own urging to plunge deeply into Jung's work. She believed when I first met her, in 1958, that she had probably plunged deeply enough into depth psychology. Joyce himself, who knew Jung's work well, refused to be analyzed by the Swiss psychologist because he feared that knowing too much about his psyche might inhibit his creative powers.

O'Connor clearly felt she needed, as a woman of letters, to push beyond the New Criticism, which in the fifties dominated the teaching of literature. Thus her letter to me in 1959, about her reaction to two teachers at Wesleyan College, is well known for its attack on New Critical methods in the classroom. After describing the heavy-handed attempts of one of the teachers to interpret her symbols, she concluded, "Anyway, that's what's happening to the teaching of literature" (*HB*, 334).

The direction in which she wanted to move appeared clear to me, finally, in 1962 when she become interested in my ideas on the way in which her novella "The Lame Shall Enter First," both completed and elucidated the meaning of *The Violent Bear It Away*. Out of her concerns with where she was headed with these two works grew a brief critical collaboration that I have described elsewhere.[6]

My collaboration with O'Connor on the problem of the diabolical in her later work was part of an upswing in our friendship. In early December 1961, at a get-together at Andalusia which included Bill and Jenny Sessions, there was a spirit of mutual good feeling between us, one which she described in part in a letter to "A": "Dr. Spivey arrived while Bill and Jenny were here and he was at his most hilarious, which entertained them and entertained him and kept me from having to entertain either of

---

[6]For my discussion of *The Violent Bear It Away* and "The Lame Shall Enter It First," see "Flannery O'Connor: Georgia's Theological Storyteller" in *The Humanities in the South*, 1-17, and "Flannery O'Connor's View of God and Man" *Studies in Short Fiction* 1 (Spring 1964): 200-206. For a discussion of my work with O'Connor in the area of literary criticism, see "Flannery O'Connor's Quest for a Critic" *Flannery O'Connor Bulletin* 15 (1968): 29-34, and "Flannery O'Connor, the New Criticism and Deconstruction" *Southern Review* 23 (April 1987): 271-81.

them" (*HB*, 458-59). My announcement to her early in 1962 of my impending marriage to Julia Douglass brought with it a lowering of feelings between us, but our relationship moved upwards again when I began to correspond with her about "The Lame Shall Enter First."

In a letter of 27 January 1963 concerning an article I had written on "The Lame Shall Enter First," O'Connor wrote me: "You have certainly got my intention down on this story . . . I'm not sure myself that I carried out the intention dramatically so well" (*HB*, 506). Then, in the next sentence of this letter, appears a note of self-doubt that can be seen growing stronger in some of her letters in 1963 and 1964, a note paralleling her growing illness leading to death in August 1964: "To tell you the truth, I haven't read the story over since it was published because I didn't want to be confronted too strongly with my failure with it" (*HB*, 506). There is in this statement a self-doubt I had not really felt in her letters and conversations before. Thus I was somewhat amazed to read these two sentences at the end of the letter: "I do thank you for writing this. It's a great help to me to know that somebody understands what I am after doing" (*HB*, 507). At this time in 1963, with some excellent critical articles beginning to appear about her work and with her own deepening sense of her emerging role as woman of letters, a role she told me in 1961 that she believed she could fill, one might well have expected expressions of hope concerning her literary accomplishments. But it was not so. On the thirtieth of March of the same year, she wrote "A" that "the one overwhelming sense I have had, constantly, is of my own inarticulateness" (*HB*, 511).

O'Connor's growing depression may well have been linked to the failure of most readers and critics to understand what she was saying in *The Violent Bear It Away*. She came to believe that her readers could not follow her into this particular dramatization of evil in the modern world. Possibly she was too caught up in her own profound mental and creative consideration of the role of a personal devil, that fallen angel whose existence she never doubted. O'Connor began to sense after 1960 that she was not entirely welcome at certain conferences on literature and religion to which she was invited. For instance, on 15 March 1963, she wrote Sally and Robert Fitzgerald about a "Symposium on Religion and Art" that she took part in at Sweet Briar College in Virginia: "[B]oy do I have a stomach full of liberal religion! The Devil had his day there" (*HB*, 510). She wrote that she "waded in and gave them a nasty dose of orthodoxy," "them" including John Ciardi and others who clearly would have had no sympathy for her orthodoxy. Ciardi ended the symposium, according to her, by declaring "why religion was no good" (*HB*, 511).

O'Connor's continuing self-doubts were continually being fuelled by a growing awareness that only a very few critics and fellow writers had the orthodox religious views that formed at least part of the intellectual basis of both her fiction and her criticism. And yet her own desire to participate as a woman of letters in literary conferences continued to be strong right up to the operation on 15 February 1964 for a benign fibroid tumor which reactivated her arrested lupus. On 18 February, she wrote Louise and Thomas Gossett: "I sure do wish I could come but I had to cancel all the lectures—Boston College, Brown, and the University of Texas" (*HB*, 566).

By 1963 O'Connor may well have begun to wonder if America had a place for such a writer and woman of letters as herself. The paradox was that, as many of her critics were distancing themselves from her theological views, they were, along with her admirers, becoming more deeply appreciative of her fiction as both art and as a repository of "Blakean" vision. But few could take literally some of her bedrock beliefs—such as the existence of a personal devil—that undergirded her vision.

As her art gained admirers after 1960, her deepest vision, that contained in *The Violent Bear It Away*, remained too formidable for most of her best readers. The irony of my own relationship with O'Connor was that as her deepest apocalyptic and theological insights were increasingly rejected, I as a former liberal Protestant came to believe increasingly in the underlying ideas of her later work, so much so that by 1962 I declared myself an Anglo-Catholic and was confirmed in the Episcopal Church, still holding out against what was for me a problem with the ecclesiastical hierarchy of the Roman Catholic Church—a problem O'Connor had done her best to solve for me in both conversation and letters. I began to see by 1962 that many of our disagreements had arisen because of my liberal and, to her, shallow Christian philosophy. But, by 1963, it was too late to continue our old battles over religion, literature, and philosophy.

Even at the end of her life, O'Connor continued to be both the Blakean apocalyptic visionary *and* the woman of letters, urbane and intellectual in spite of her mask of the Southern rustic. Robert Fitzgerald had written that with the translation of *Wise Blood* into French in 1956 she "found herself now and henceforward a woman-of-letters." He also stated, quite truthfully, that "she and her devoted and keenwitted mother, who learned thoroughly to understand what Flannery was up to, became an effective team" (*ERMC*, xxii). Indeed had she lived longer, O'Connor would have managed well as both writer and woman of letters. The truth of her vision, however, was something deeper, stranger, and more unfathomable than we yet know. I prefer to think of her as an emerging woman of letters, one not fully established at the end of her life, as eventually she would have been had she lived longer. She was the "Blakean" visionary that Gordon had called her, and she needed, as true visionaries do, time by herself, a loneliness to cultivate her strange vision. It may well be that the complexity of her rich gifts caused problems both personal and artistic that were more difficult to solve than Robert Fitzgerald suggested. What I would now like to suggest in the analysis of her vision that follows is that though she was a gifted critic, thinker, artist, and even woman of letters, she was primarily a literary visionary not unlike Joyce or even Dostoevski.

III.
The Visionary

Chapter 5

The Writer as Young Prophet

One of the chief paradoxes of the life and literary career of Flannery O'Connor is summed up in the image of Hazel Motes, the protagonist of her first extended work, the novel *Wise Blood*. Although she was the exact opposite of Haze in almost all ways personal, the protagonist of *Wise Blood* is the essential prophet that lived in the heart of the young woman from Milledgeville. Like Haze Motes, O'Connor, as an essentially religious writer, very early had spiritually decamped from the old Agrarian Southern past to find a new life in a modern city. Her move to New York was, in part, an effort to escape an inherited repressive puritanism and also an attempt to discover long-neglected and even largely forgotten experiences that by the time she had written the stories in her last book, *Everything That Rises Must Converge*, she saw as basic to Christianity in particular and religion in general. Thus Haze and other prophetic figures who would appear in later works represented various aspects of O'Connor's continuing personal and literary efforts to create visions of a kind of religious experience that would effectively bind isolated individuals into a meaningful community. Her continuing visionary quest from *Wise Blood* to the end of her literary career was to present metaphors of the search for an authentic community based on love and on visionary insight.

Just as James Joyce sought to establish for himself a life's role as a prophetic artist in *A Portrait of the Artist as a Young Man*, Flannery O'Connor in *Wise Blood* was seeking a role for herself as both prophet and artist. Both Joyce and O'Connor sought first in early short stories to establish for themselves a sense of their own milieu, and then in a first short novel to explore ways in which they would proceed to record their visions of a modern world that was at once dying and seeking to be reborn. To discuss O'Connor or Joyce separate from their literary visions is to risk ignoring what was most basic to them. For the two authors the need to be both artist and prophet was so great, the drive for literary accomplishment so deep, that personality in itself became of secondary importance. For both the continuing need for personal development at times seemed unimportant in comparison with their visionary-artistic calling; the result of this need was, as with many great artists, occasional lapses into a certain harshness of temperament.

O'Connor's editor and publisher, Robert Giroux, saw immediately upon meeting the young author whom Robert Lowell had brought to his New York office in February of 1949 a strength and drive to achieve literary significance. "Behind her soft-spoken speech, clear-eyed gaze, and shy manner," Giroux wrote, "I sensed a tremendous strength. This was the rarest kind of young writer, one who was prepared to work her utmost and knew exactly what she must do with her talent" (CS, viii). Giroux saw immediately behind the shy mask of a twenty-three-year-old woman the kind of stamina and determination exhibited by her mother and her many Irish relatives who had carved out for themselves a large place among the Southern gentry in two rigidly stratified small Southern cities, Savannah and Milledgeville. He saw that quality of the aristocratic sense of herself, an attitude that she summed up in her statement that anyone who knows who he or she is can go anywhere. This is O'Connor the insider, the non-alienated Southern lady I have already written of, the woman becoming more personally powerful every year as she became, very early, a successful serious writer and then an emerging woman of letters whose lectures were well received in colleges and universities in various parts of the country. But the great paradox of her life is that the outsider aspect of O'Connor was an even more significant part of her makeup than the tough insider quality that served her so well in her struggle to make her vision known to the world.

Giroux also went to the heart of this outsider quality of O'Connor when he wrote, comparing her with her chief admirer among Catholic writers, Thomas Merton: "The aura of aloneness surrounding each of them was not an accident. It was their métier, in which they refined and deepened their very different talents in a short span of time. They both died at the height of their powers" (CS, xiii). Giroux does not say exactly what their métier was, but from their best work we know it was their ability to withdraw deeply into themselves and to bring forth visions of the authentic community. They were, in effect, modern shamans. Fittingly, in the mid-fifties when O'Connor was becoming an established American writer, one of the most popular books among intellectuals in England and America was Colin Wilson's *The Outsider*, an essay that deals in part with the shamanic aspects of existentialists like Albert Camus. Evidence does not exist that O'Connor knew Wilson's work, but the large reception of *The Outsider* and subsequent works by Wilson indicates the depth of concern at that time for the subject of the visionary aspects of modern literature. Wilson's book, coupled with the growing popularity of Teilhard de Chardin, indicates a growing climate of opinion that O'Connor herself would tap into in order to bring forth visions in her later work of the possibilities of the renewal of communal life through the visionary experience.

The visionary side of O'Connor is not so much summed up in the *Wise Blood*'s protagonist Haze Motes as it is in the boy Enoch Emery, who tells his new friend Motes that he has "wise blood." O'Connor once wrote "A" that she was in a sense all of her characters. She also wrote this of herself and Enoch Emery: "Enoch didn't care so much for New York. He said there wasn't any privacy there. Every time he went to sit in the bushes there was already somebody ahead of him."[1] Ironically, O'Connor would use the word "blood" to symbolize the intuitive visionary side of life in much the same way in which D. H. Lawrence used the term. In consciously expressing her dislike of Lawrence and of other intuitive writers like Wolfe, Williams, and McCullers, O'Connor, as I have earlier suggested concerning her inability to fully escape her inherited puritanism, sometimes repressed the intuitive and sexual side of her own nature. Yet Enoch, the book's central character in many ways, represents an aspect of what Gordon called O'Connor's Blakean vision.

Like Blake, and also Lawrence, who resembles Blake in many ways, O'Connor possessed visionary qualities that were deeply feminine, qualities that were earthy, sexual, and communal. Her visionary nature was not that of Catholics like Saint Teresa or Dante, who were both involved with their everyday existence but who were also individuals capable of profound glimpses of heaven and hell. Very little in O'Connor's vision seems sky-pointed—for her the Virgin Mary never appears—yet, like Teilhard, the modern Catholic visionary who figures most deeply in her work, she quite naturally anchored her "blood" feelings in the world around her. Yet she was no less a visionary than earlier Catholic mystics who looked to the sky for inspiration. Her mysticism instead was directed at nature and society, and with the term "blood" she suggested a kind of wisdom that springs from sources we associate with nonrational aspects of the mind.

---

[1]Beth Dawkins Bassett, "Converging Lines," *Emory Magazine* 58/4 (April 1982): 18.

Robert Giroux revealed a deep awareness of the Enoch Emery side of O'Connor when he wrote that "Flannery had less vanity than anyone I have ever known" (CS, xii). I encountered in her a listening, quiet side that seemed to be unaware of ego demands, but this was not the usual O'Connor one saw. More often than not, when she was at home in Andalusia, she was the insider I have already described as well as the O'Connor of the lecture circuit, the emerging woman of letters in the literary symposium or the question-and-answer session. With an interviewer she could be very strong-minded indeed, exhibiting the pride one may well expect of most writers in such situations. The letters, of course, reveal the determined quality of a hard-nosed critic and intellectual. But the strangely silent and waiting O'Connor, seemingly free of vanity, was often present just behind the insider's mask. Giroux, in noting that *Wise Blood* was indeed a strange book, quoted the original publisher's letter to the effect that he had "sensed a kind of aloneness in the book." Giroux then quoted O'Connor's reply that " 'I am not writing a conventional novel, and I think the quality of the novel I write will derive precisely from the peculiarity of aloneness, if you like, of the experience I write from' " (CS, x).

The "aloneness" springs primarily from the fact that O'Connor in her first major fictional effort was seeking to come to terms with the two aspects of herself represented by Haze and Enoch in order to capture through their eyes the association of both certain individuals and of the societies in which they lived. In the deepest sense I think O'Connor was trying to come to terms with both the masculine and feminine aspects of herself—with the anima-animus dualism contained within everyone. Anthony Burgess, writing in the sixties, discussed this struggle with the opposites of anima and animus found in writers like Muriel Spark and Iris Murdoch that O'Connor sometimes admired: "The novelist is a hermaphrodite, prefigured in the Greek myth of the seer Teiresias."[2] He further wrote of those women novelists who seek to hold in tension the masculine and feminine aspects of themselves: "And yet we recognize two distinct, opposite, and complementary poles in the novel, which we can designate by the Chinese terms *yin* and *yang*—the feminine and masculine poles in a presexual . . . sense."[3] Unlike Murdoch or Spark, however, O'Connor was never able to sustain for long this tension of

---

[2]Burgess, *The Novel Now* (New York: Pegasus, 1967) 119.
[3]Ibid.

opposites. The reason was, I believe, that her conscious religious concerns, growing out of both a conservative Catholicism based on her
reading in Aquinas and on that apocalyptic Catholicism she found in
Guardini, Bernanos, and Picard, led her in *Wise Blood* and succeeding
works to concentrate on the masculine side of herself in her quest to
establish in contemporary fiction the basis for a Roman Catholic apocalyptic prophecy. Yet the most powerful side of *Wise Blood* and of her
later fiction dealing with modern fundamentalist prophets grew out of her
Blakean imagination, a side of herself that she, at least consciously, often
felt uncomfortable with. She rejected, even violently, the Blakean prophetic qualities of Thomas Wolfe and D. H. Lawrence and also felt uncomfortable with the spontaneous and often powerful symbolism of William
Faulkner and Virginia Woolf, and yet she felt deeply the need to establish a prophetic fictional persona in order to declare her own vision.

Just as Dante prepared himself for his major work with an evocation
of the power of that feminine image of Beatrice which undergirded his
Commedia and as Joyce had to invoke the image of the autonomous artist
in *A Portrait of the Artist as a Young Man*, so O'Connor had to encounter the powers of the fundamentalist prophet who would renounce a
desacralized world to encounter the mysteries of God. It might at first
seem that I am putting O'Connor on too high a pedestal in relating her
works to those of Dante and Joyce. Yet both were her masters. As a
Roman Catholic and a prophetic visionary, she consciously invoked both
and plumbed in her own intuitive way the work of both of these literary
giants. But it well may be that her own literary problems might have
been related to her struggle to establish a deep working relationship with
the anima and animus in the tradition of Dante and Joyce. Not only did
Dante encounter the power of the feminine in the figure of Beatrice, but
he also had a firm grip on the image of his own masculinity in his persona. And though Joyce addressed himself as male artist, he also deeply
and consciously grasped the power of the feminine in both his early and
later work.

O'Connor, in the character of Haze and later in young Tarwater,
established the figure of the masculine prophet struggling with his own
nihilism as well as with his gradually unfolding powers of prophecy, but,
through the character of Enoch Emory, she presented in *Wise Blood* a
denunciation of the largely defeminized social scene that the modern
world has become. The world as seen through the eyes of Enoch is one
in which women and children are shown to be powerless and therefore

somehow deserving of the isolation they are subjected to. The nature of
Enoch's world, which partly reflects O'Connor's own personal world, is
one which a child cannot understand but one which the discerning reader
can see—through O'Connor's visionary metaphors—to be the result of
the crushing weight of white masculine authority and power upon powerless women, children, and blacks.

In *Wise Blood*, the prophetic principle contained within Haze represents O'Connor's own attempt to establish herself as a religious artist
who in a visionary manner stated what was for her the only way the
blighted modern world could be healed: by letting the autonomous will
admit its failures and accept God's grace. But the deepest imaginative
power of *Wise Blood* is to be found in O'Connor's vision of a secularized, power-oriented world that needs healing. It has taken some years
for critics to catch up with the intensity of her vision. To grasp the complexity of *Wise Blood*, it is necessary to see how she tied together Haze's
groping for a prophetic role and Enoch's vision of a world that denies
meaningful roles to most women and to all children.

In his 1976 critical study, *The Pruning Word: The Parables of Flannery O'Connor*, John R. May stated from the viewpoint of traditional
Catholicism that "Haze's simple language reflects of course the theological sophistication of his creator."[4] One of the literary revelations we
find in O'Connor is her insight into the ability of simple people to plunge
to the heart of theological and philosophical problems; in fact, no one in
American literature has shown more skill in realistically presenting
complex ideas in the simple language of the unlettered. By the end of
Wise Blood, Haze begins to emerge as the kind of prophet O'Connor
sought to establish as a character in modern letters. In his study of O'Connor, May revealed a profound awareness of the way that Haze reflects the
concepts of a nihilistic existentialism in order to discover at least some
aspects of the role of the religious prophet. Thus May stated that
"O'Connor understood that the prophet interprets events in the light of
the covenant, announcing God's judgment of the people's sins and His
call to fidelity."[5] May also stated concisely the meaning of Haze's self-
blinding and of his medieval penance: "[H]is ritual blinding is a preference for the darkness of mystery over the nihilism of blasphemous

---

[4]John R. May, *The Pruning Word: The Parables of Flannery O'Connor* (Notre Dame
IL: Notre Dame University Press, 1976) 134.
[5]Ibid., 17.

self-sufficiency; his penitential stones and barbed wire an acceptance of his unfinished nature against the absurd denial of human limitation."[6] Yet May missed the point O'Connor was making about "wise blood," a symbol denoting the child's and the woman's visionary awareness of both human suffering and human happiness. "To boast of 'wise blood' is," May argued, "in the final analysis, the ultimate human folly."[7] What May failed to see, like so many others who have praised O'Connor for the theological side of her fiction, is that *Wise Blood* is, in part, a tragedy.

Haze's death is foreshadowed by his separation from Enoch. They need each other; one without the other is doomed to failure. Without the masculine guidance of a theological Haze, Enoch can never rise above his involvement with the flesh. Enoch is last seen dressed as a gorilla. And, without Enoch, Haze is cut off from the wellsprings of happiness that the company of Enoch brought him. He is becoming as morose as those "prophets" of his childhood that he had been trying all his life to escape. Without the help of that part of his makeup represented by Enoch and in fact activated by this character, Haze cannot continue his prophetic work.

O'Connor in the preface to the second edition of *Wise Blood* called her first major work a "comic novel," but the premature death of Hazel undoubtedly gives it a tragic turn. *Tragicomedy* is unquestionably a better word to use for *Wise Blood*. The tragic aspects of the novel, together with the social criticism found in the work, make most readers, in spite of obvious humorous moments, see the work's tragic dimensions as being paramount. With its mood of "aloneness," which the book's first publisher's reader noted and which O'Connor herself said the novel possessed, *Wise Blood* resembles a work like Kafka's *The Trial* far more than any ordinary "comic" novel, even one like Mark Twain's *Huckleberry Finn*, with which it has been compared. Kafka's fiction, which friends of the author found humorous when he read it in manuscript, indeed contains a strange element of the absurd, an element O'Connor herself helped introduce into contemporary American fiction. The absurdist element in *Wise Blood,* like that in Kafka's work, causes the reader to have a strong awareness of the isolation of individuals who are caught up in social situations beyond their control.

---

[6]Ibid., 137.
[7]Ibid.

Except for Stanley Edgar Hyman and a few others who have noted that O'Connor borrowed extensively in *Wise Blood* from her early mentor Nathanael West, O'Connor's critics for several decades now have kept their minds focused primarily on the theological aspects of her work and have ignored her often sweeping social criticism that took into full account the ravages of contemporary sexism and racism as well as the debilitating effects of worn-out and often destructive religious zealots. O'Connor herself, with often telling remarks about her own work, led critics away from aspects of her work that she herself tended to ignore. In strong, conscious efforts to establish herself as an artist writing about what she sometimes called the "religious individual," O'Connor seemed to suppress any mention of some of the most basic elements in her work, and those of her critics who are conservative Catholics or Protestants have joined her in focusing on certain aspects of her religious fiction to the almost total exclusion of other elements.

What has long been needed is a school of O'Connor criticism that explores in depth the modernist elements in the writer's work without neglecting her religious and philosophical viewpoint. A significant work of the late eighties, Suzanne Paulson's *Flannery O'Connor: A Study of the Short Fiction*, helped to highlight neglected aspects of modernism in O'Connor's fiction. Rejecting the overriding religious concerns of Robert Drake, for instance, who has written that O'Connor has only "one story to tell," Paulson presented a comprehensive view of the author's vision of the many aspects of the modern tragedy of the suppression of numerous individuals and of many groups who have been discriminated against in the first half of the twentieth century.[8] In seeking what she called "a more balanced approach than the strictly theological one that dominates most criticism on O'Connor today," Paulson noted, among the author's many modernist themes, the undermining in a "scientific/industrial world" of "the human capacity for meaningful relationships." Individuals are defined "not in terms of spirituality but as animals, or worse, machines."[9] Furthermore, Paulson noted that O'Connor's fiction presents "class conflicts, racial differences, and the mindless conformity of groups marching in processions or parades and basing their sense of

---

[8]Robert Drake, *Flannery O'Connor: A Critical Essay* (Grand rapids MI: William B. Eerdmans, 1966) 17.

[9]Suzanne M. Paulson, *Flannery O'Connor: A Study of the Short Fiction* (Boston: Twayne Publishers, 1988) ix.

identity on such status symbols as uniforms, possessions, skin color, and the Christian faith."[10]

In speaking of O'Connor's Blakean vision, Caroline Gordon primarily had in mind the Georgia writer's spiritual insight. But, as with Blake, this insight is closely connected to social dislocation and blatant injustice. Behind Blake's vision of social dislocation is a will to power that separates and divides people, causing a few to withdraw into their property and affluence and others to be left separated, isolated, and without knowledge of how they can ever find their way into authentic social relationships. Enoch Emery is O'Connor's chief symbol of the dispossessed. With only a few weeks of education in the Rodemill Boys' Bible Academy, Enoch lacks the knowledge for finding his way in a Southern city that seems to lack any kind of social cohesion. He is thrown back on his intuition, his "wise blood" as he calls it, but it is not enough to help him find the life he seeks. It does, however, guide him to Haze Motes, who has survived four years of war in order to become what in the years after World War II would be thought of as an "adult male." And yet Haze's adulthood is in many ways only a surface matter. What it is to be a "man" still puzzles him just as what his proper relationship to the opposite sex should be remains for him a mystery. Yet Haze, as Enoch's wise blood seems to tell him, is at least looking for a way to overcome the intense isolation of a society in which everyone seems to be working for himself or herself alone. In seeking to create his own religion, Haze is endeavoring to find that principle inherent in the very word *religion*, that is, a principle that will effectively bind people into a creative unity.

In the characters of Enoch and Haze, O'Connor invested a powerful sense of what Robert Giroux called "aloneness." When we first see both characters they are caught up in this quality of "aloneness" and have accepted it by divesting themselves of their rural past in their acceptance of the city as the only true abode of the modern individual. But Enoch, in his need to move beyond his "aloneness" and the very atmosphere of isolation instilled by the city, attaches himself to Haze, for more than any other reason, because he is determined to find a way out of "aloneness."

Theological critics of O'Connor have generally seen Haze as a kind of Christian prophet, "a Christian *malgré lui*," as the author herself called him in the preface to the second edition. But O'Connor, neither in this

---

[10]Ibid., xii.

preface nor anywhere else, took into full account the intensity of Haze's revolt against the Christianity he had experienced. It was probably best for her that she did not, though I think eventually she would have taken into full account Haze's movement beyond a Christianity that had become, for many young people after World War II, either a terrifying memory or, at the other extreme, a soporific. She, of course, partly understood this aspect of her work, but theological critics have accepted her words about prophecy and Christianity without seeing that Haze and Enoch both reject their Christian past and never find a substitute for its loss, though they both are continually seeking one.

Haze, nevertheless, is a prophet because he has been trained to be one by his grandfather. But, as a prophet, his first task is to clear away the ruins of his debased Protestant past. In order to create his own personal religion, which he discovers for himself through his "prophetic" preaching in the streets of the city of Taulkinham, Haze must eliminate Christ, its central figure, along with theological terms like *justification* and *sanctification*. He first felt the need to reject his religious past when he was in the army. Thus he reacts to the casual sins of his army buddies: "All he wanted was to believe them and get rid of it once and for all, and he saw the opportunity here to get rid of it without corruption, to be converted to nothing instead of to evil" (*WB*, 24). The key word here is "corruption" because for Haze the old religion of his grandfather made the corruptions of death and hell so powerful that the boy had lived in an overpowering state of fear until he met young men in the army who believed that words like "evil" and "hell" were meaningless abstractions from a dead past. Haze's grandfather and the Tennessee mountain community which he represented had kept their religious fundamentalism alive in order to blot out their sense of isolation from the rest of the world. Yet his experience of the loneliness of the modern city had resurrected in Haze the need for a religious reality to replace this fundamentalist Christianity.

Theological interpreters of O'Connor's work have often seen *Wise Blood* as an attack on the ferocity of certain aspects of Southern fundamentalism, but O'Connor as a Catholic and a literary follower of Joyce was aware that Catholics also had been affected in the twentieth century by too great an emphasis on hell in the previous century. The Catholic historian Paul Johnson wrote: "It was the redemptorists who, in 1807, resurrected a remarkable seventeenth-century work by F. Pinamonti, *Hell*

Opened to Christians, and reprinted it with horrific woodcuts."[11] Johnson further noted that an edition of this work was published in Ireland as late as 1889 and that "it has demonstrable links with the sermon on Hell described in James Joyce's *Portrait of the Artist as a Young Man*. . . . Redemptorists often preached Hell-sermons at Catholic schools."[12]

Just as Joyce showed the young Dedalus struggling to free himself from the sense of hell that he inherited from his religious schooling, so O'Connor revealed a young Haze Motes tearing himself away from his own early training in a fundamentalism whose ferocious Jesus is described by his grandfather as being "soul-hungry." The grandfather himself is "a waspish old man who had ridden over three counties with Jesus hidden in his head like a stinger" (*WB*, 20). Haze, like Joyce's Dedalus, is early haunted by thoughts of both death and hell. Like Dedalus, Haze feels called to be a cleric, but, also like Dedalus, Haze is overcome by fear and revulsion springing from his encounter with the power of God's representative on earth, a power generally used to hurt, to threaten, to condemn, above all to summon pictures to the mind of the total corruption of body and soul. There is, of course, a link between the authority and power that priests and preachers possess in the work of Joyce and O'Connor and their pictures of the horrors of hell and human corruption. Paul Johnson stated, concerning the growing authoritarianism of nineteenth-century Catholicism: "The stress on authority, and the maintenance of detailed clerical control of the conscience of the individual, were almost necessarily accompanied by a continued insistence on eternal punishment."[13] He added, "The nearer a man moved to Rome, the more the need for Hell seemed to increase (though it was also marked on the extreme fundamentalist wing of Protestantism)."[14]

In the backwoods of the East Tennessee community from which Haze sprang, Christianity as well as the Southern mountain culture itself is passing from the scene just as the old Ireland was passing away before Joyce's own eyes. Haze and Dedalus both must push toward some city that has divested itself of the old male-oriented religious authority that was dying with frenzied presentations of human corruption. Even attempts at presenting a view of salvation created fear for Catholics and

---

[11]Paul Johnson, *A History of Christianity* (New York: Atheneum, 1987) 383.
[12]Ibid.
[13]Ibid., 382.
[14]Ibid.

fundamentalists. Thus, when Enoch first encounters Haze in Taulkinham, he describes his reason for the rejection of "a lot of Jesus business." After four weeks in the Rodemill Boys' Bible Academy, he says, "I thought I was going to be sanctified crazy" (*WB*, 44). Like Haze, Enoch has lost family, religion, and community. He had only four weeks of religious teaching, and it was too much for him. His loss of family and his entry into the Bible Academy are presented by O'Connor with an irony and an economy typical of her style: "Thisyer woman that traded me from my daddy she sent me. She was a Welfare woman" (*WB*, 44). Because he has found nothing to relieve him from his isolation in religion, family, education, or the welfare service, Enoch turns to Haze because he senses in him a human quality that reaches out to others as well as a sense of purposefulness that suggests it is possible in the city to make for oneself a way of life.

Haze, in fact, does have a purpose when he comes to Taulkinham, which is to seek a new life beyond the dying rural communities of his youth, with their worn-out religion and their fixations on the corruption of the body and the cult of the funeral which had held his mind entranced as he grew up. What Haze seeks in the city is a positive life force, a power to make him forget his earlier orientation toward hell and death. Like Joyce's Dedalus, he seeks the life force in women. For Dedalus and Haze, the religion of their youth has been associated with male authority figures who seemed to deny the feminine principle. For Haze all power in Eastrod, Tennessee, is in the hands of men; his own mother seems to be a person of little consequence, emotionally and culturally starved as she is. Eastrod is a hard-bitten mountain community of white Protestant fanatics which has preserved most of its pioneer masculine beliefs. But these beliefs are dying among the young as the city beckons them to a new life.

The city of Taulkinham, connected as it is with the plantation South, presents to Haze images of various forms of feminine power. In the army Haze had tried to maintain his grandfather's religious beliefs, but eventually he gave in to his fellow soldiers anti-metaphysical views. Later he accepted their approach to a debased vision of the feminine principle, which O'Connor summed up in one sentence: "They told him he didn't have any soul and left for their brothel" (*WB*, 24). Haze's first action upon arriving in Taulkinham is to seek out a prostitute. Like Joyce's Dedalus, the flight from religion and God leads Haze to the feminine mysteries thought to be embodied in harlots. But in his first encounter with the mystery of profane sex, Haze finds himself overwhelmed by a woman who appears far more powerful than he is. Indeed, he seems to be confronting a mother figure, a fact that causes him to protest: " 'What I mean to have you know is: I'm no goddam preacher' " (*WB*, 34). Mrs. Watts, the prostitute, readily accepts his need for mothering:

> Mrs. Watts eyed him steadily with only a slight smirk. Then she put her other hand under his face and tickled it in a motherly way. "That's okay, son," she said. "Momma don't care if you ain't a preacher" (*WB*, 34).

However, while Haze was asleep, Mrs. Watts "got up and cut the top of his hat out in an obscene shape" (*WB*, 110). This gesture is obviously an attack on his masculinity. As Steven Olson has demonstrated, the hat for O'Connor is a symbol of the young backwoods male's sense of selfhood and masculine energy.[15] Haze thus reacts against Mrs. Watts: "He felt that he should have a woman, not for the sake of the pleasure in her, but to prove that he didn't believe in sin since he practiced what was called it" (*WB*, 110).

In seeking to overcome his own drive to immerse himself in a femininity that would free him from the isolation of his entire life, Haze next turns to a young woman who is, without his knowing it, stalking him. The girl, Sabbath Lily Hawks, is the daughter of one of those phony evangelists who seem to flourish in Taulkinham, a type O'Connor satirizes mercilessly in her fiction. Asa Hawks poses as a blind prophet, but there is something sinister and destructive about him, a destructiveness he shares with his daughter, whom Haze at first sees as an innocent. Having escaped the all-embracing Mrs. Watts, in his next woman, Sabbath Lily, Haze hopes to assert his masculinity by creating a disciple who will follow the beliefs of his new church without Christ: "He wanted someone he could teach something to and he took it for granted that the blind man's child, since she was so homely, would also be innocent" (*WB*, 110).

In one of the most uproarious sexual adventures in contemporary literature, Haze begins his absurd courtship of Sabbath, and he finds out how weak his stunted masculinity really is when he confronts in her a

---

[15]Steven Olson, "Tarwater's Hats," *Studies in the Literary Imagination* 20/2 (Fall 1987): 37-51.

sexual hunger that drains him for a time of all energy and nearly wrecks his nerves. He discovers that behind her mask of innocence and her sinister father's mask of piety is a destructive power that is a measure of the psychic hunger of Taulkinham, a city where seemingly endless talk masks a terrible need for human relationships beyond those springing from the lust for money and sex. This lust is often symbolized by animals in *Wise Blood*; animal lust for O'Connor symbolizes the decline of humanity into postures resembling those of apes and jackals.

Taulkinham in its size and shape reminds us of a city near Milledgeville, which is Macon, Georgia, but it more deeply was inspired by the few months O'Connor spent in Atlanta in 1941, where she attended North Fulton High School at the same time as the poet James Dickey. In fact, she once pointed out to me that her portrait of the zoo—a key symbol in *Wise Blood*—was drawn directly from the Grant Park Zoo in Atlanta. In using Macon and Atlanta both as a setting for *Wise Blood*, John Huston in his excellent cinematic interpretation of the book revealed a profound understanding of O'Connor's absurdist vision of cities as she knew them in the thirties and early forties.

Haze is saved by his prophetic mission from being turned into an empty shell by Sabbath's sexual demands. By summoning his remaining masculine energies, the young prophet escapes Sabbath, much as the medieval Saint Thomas supposedly drove off with a hot poker a prostitute (see O'Connor's 28 August 1955 letter to "A" on this subject). But his prophetic work finally collapses when he falls into the hands of another fake evangelist, Hoover Shoats. The result is that he murders Hoover's replacement for him. Haze's prophetic mission collapses when he is overcome by his inner rage. His powers seemingly fail him in his quest for a religious vocation of his own making. The result is that he falls permanently into the hands of another mother substitute, Mrs. Flood. In this owner and manager of a boarding house we see the old hierarchical Southern female of the plantation South. Like Haze, she too has been dispossessed of her rural past and has had to make do in a nondescript city. Unlike Haze, she has no message. Her house is one great womb that seeks to suck into itself as much money as possible. Mrs. Flood has the blind drive to renew her once glowing, now largely forgotten heritage; her conscious set of beliefs now consist of prejudices against the federal government as well as against the blacks and foreigners that she believes government officials have given her tax money to:

She felt that the money she paid out in taxes returned to all the worth-less pockets in the world, that the government not only sent it to foreign niggers and a-rabs, but wasted it at home on blind fools and on every idiot who could sign his name on a card (*WB*, 214).

Her lust for money is as strong as Sabbath's sexual lust: "She couldn't look at anything steadily without wanting it" (*WB*, 214). Once she felt she had owned everything, but now her life must be spent in getting back some of what was lost: "She felt justified in getting anything at all back that she could, money or anything else, as if she had once owned the earth and been dispossessed of it" (*WB*, 214).

Paulson has stated that the "masculinization of culture and a revul-sion for femininity" is a major aspect of the many male/female conflicts in O'Connor's fiction.[16] Certainly the city of Taulkinham is dominated by a masculine spirit that seeks ever increasing aggrandizement in monetary, religious, sexual, and racial areas; yet, in *Wise Blood*, the primary dichotomy of power is between those who are caught up in the yang principle of activity versus those who, like young Enoch with his wise blood, are primarily oriented toward the emotional, intuitive, receptive principle represented by the Chinese principle of yin. Without knowing what he is doing, Haze seeks relationships with the feminine powers of creativity, partly in order to achieve, unconsciously of course, a balance within himself between yin and yang. But having grown up in an overly masculinized society in East Tennessee and then having served through-out the war in an almost totally masculinized army, he possesses no wisdom concerning the nature of the masculine and feminine principles. The result is that he is always seeking the yin, or feminine, principle in women who are activated by a yang principle that has become essentially possessive and therefore destructive. Thus Hazel in his blindness is drawn to the destructive sexuality of Mrs. Watts and Sabbath. Recoiling from these two women who represent the feminine principle become destruc-tive, Haze turns at last to a mother figure in Mrs. Flood, only to discover that he is in the grasp of a possessive hierarchical Southern female who intends to use him for her own purposes. Caught between destructive sex and destructive motherhood, Haze attempts, unsuccessfully, to establish his masculinity through a series of destructive acts of his own.

---

[16]Paulson, *Flannery O'Connor*, xii.

Haze was forced by his army buddies and his own fear and loathing of his early religious teachings to give up his metaphysical beliefs, but he has nevertheless accepted the vocation of preacher foisted upon him by his grandfather. Haze has inherited the modern American male's belief that he can express his masculinity only through his occupation. The corollary of this proposition is that the male's relationship with females is based on the dominance associated with his particular job—the more money and power associated with the job, the more dominance. Haze as preacher then creates his own non-metaphysical religion, denying the reality of God and Jesus as Savior, which he preaches not so much to convert others as to find his own masculinity in a male-dominated city. Instead of the despised cross of Christ, which symbolizes suffering, submission to God, and concern for others above one's self, Haze takes for his chief sacrament the automobile: " 'Nobody with a good car needs to be justified' " (*WB*, 113). The car provides a symbol that declares the death of God and all God's sacraments. It is more than simply a symbol; it is an actual means of fleeing all theologies and sacraments. After he has bought his car, Haze announces triumphantly: " 'I knew when I first saw it that it was the car for me, and since I've had it, I've had a place to be that I can always get away in' " (*WB*, 115). To get away, to keep moving, not to look back because, as an American baseball player has said, somebody might be gaining on you—these are, for Haze, the actions of Americans who are truly modern. And he believes that it remains for him to codify and preach the theology of the new post-World War II city. His preaching is remarkably clear in stating the new church's straight-forward theology:

> Well, I preach the Church Without Christ. I'm a member and preacher to that church where the blind don't see and the lame don't walk and what's dead stays that way. Ask me about that church and I'll tell you it's the church that the blood of Jesus don't fool with redemption (*WB*, 105).

Only a few other points are needed to fill out Haze's theology: " '[T]here was no Fall because there was nothing to fall from and no Redemption because there was no Fall and no Judgment because there wasn't the first two. Nothing mattered but that Jesus was a liar" (*WB*, 105). For Haze, who has, in part at least, given up the old Southern racism, Jesus is also a "trick on niggers." Religion for Haze is one way that the secularized religious hierarchy has kept the proletariat in servitude.

Haze Motes has often been compared with various existentialists like Sartre and Nietzsche. But Sartre was filled with old-fashioned secular idealism about improving society whereas Haze believes that flight from society is the one essential idealism. Marion Montgomery called Haze a modern Nietzsche, but the German philosopher is religious compared with Haze.[17] Nietzsche substitutes another god—Dionysus—for the dead God of Israel. Actually Haze's theology most resembles that found in Aldous Huxley's *Brave New World*, where a non-metaphysical pseudo-religion has as its chief symbol the automobile. Henry Ford is Huxley's secular god, and religious instincts are sublimated in a pseudo-mass in which chocolate malts replace the blood of Christ.

If O'Connor had continued to show in other writing the development of Haze's secular religion—or materialistic pseudo-religion, if one likes—then she would have been working in the spirit of *Brave New World*, but in fact there is a dramatic reversal in Haze's career. The reversal appears when Haze discovers that his work as secular prophet, carried on in the individualistic tradition of his rural grandfather, is meaningless in Taulkinham, where prophecy, like all other activities, is essentially a group activity whose common denominator is money. Hoover Shoats, a symbol of this modern "evangelism," tries to take Haze under his wing and teach him a materialistic religion that is unlike his own automobile-centered belief. Hoover's evangelism is based on the deceptive use of the old Christian symbols in order to induce a drugged state of "happiness," a kind of "positive thinking" needed to make converts "feel good" about themselves and the world around them. When Hoover finds Haze intractable, he hires another "evangelist" to take his place, a man named Solace Layfield. Solace, O'Connor wrote, "had consumption and a wife and six children and being a Prophet was as much work as he wanted to do" (*WB*, 201).

Haze is enraged at Solace because, as he tells the consumptive evangelist, "You ain't true . . . you believe in Jesus" (*WB*, 203). Haze's anger at both the man's hypocrisy and his belief in Jesus drives him to kill Solace, whose name suggests his sellout to the modern use of religion as a solace, a comfort, a relaxing drug that makes bearable the loneliness of the city. Haze learned from his grandfather that the work of prophecy meant struggle and honesty and the acceptance of loneliness. Haze gives

---

[17]Marion Montgomery, *Why Flannery O'Connor Stayed at Home* (LaSalle IL: Sherwood Sugden and Co., 1981) 397-409.

up his role as prophet by turning to medieval acts of penance of the sort he practiced as a child. These acts lead at last to blinding himself. He seeks through physical blindness to remove the spiritual motes in his eyes that make it impossible for him to see the larger realm of the spirit. I think O'Connor's analysis of these final actions of Haze is very much to the point in explaining what he is doing by his acts of penance. His grandfather taught him that the prophet, above all else, has integrity. By practicing a medieval form of penitence, Haze declares his integrity, and it is an integrity that leads him, in a confused way, to accept that "ragged figure of Christ" who "moves from tree to tree in the back of his mind," as O'Connor put it in the preface to the second edition of *Wise Blood*. In this preface the author summed up the book's chief theme: "For the author Hazel's integrity lies in his not being able to [get rid of the figure of Jesus in his unconscious mind]." This statement by O'Connor, I believe, needs some amplification because she did not herself understand clearly her own Blakean vision.

What motivates Haze to give up his work as a prophet is his need to discover what it is that a prophet really should be doing. He had begun his prophecy with the idea of helping people get rid of the guilt and fear caused by earlier religions; thus, by accepting a totally materialistic picture of the world, with the automobile as the basic mythic fact of this world, Haze would teach a way of escaping urban loneliness and a way of feeling important in a city that made deep personal commitments impossible. In this world the chief ritual would be always leaving where one might temporarily reside and, with the help of the car, indulging continually in brief sexual encounters. Haze, however, found that his new religion failed him. His car collapsed, the sexual encounters were painful, and his prophecy involved destructive encounters with other prophets seeking to make money from preaching a soporific Jesus who would make people "feel good." His prophetic function even serves to alienate him from his one friend, Enoch Emery, who becomes a symbol of the loss of his own human warmth and intuition, that feminine side of himself summed up in the term "wise blood." Enoch himself at last gives up on people altogether and tries to identify with a gorilla. The pain of personal commitment drives Enoch to seek lost purity and love among animals.

Facing his own failures, Haze does what people with a religious calling have often done in the past, particularly in the Catholic Church. He mortifies the flesh and retreats for a time in order to come to terms with his deepest self. For O'Connor that deepest self was Christ, but Haze never fully encounters this figure because the deceptions of Mrs. Flood mislead him in the end. Her boarding house is his place of retreat for mortification and meditation, but, just as he never grasps how deeply Taulkinham believes in money and sex, he never grasps the avarice and lust with which Mrs. Flood views him.

Mrs. Flood, O'Connor wrote, "was not religious or morbid, for which every day she thanked her stars" (*WB*, 211). Yet she sees nothing wrong with preaching. She tells Haze he ought to go back to preaching: " 'You certainly ought to start it again. It would give you something to do' " (*WB*, 221). He replies that he does not have time for preaching; in his acts of mortification, including his self-blinding, he is devoting himself to an inward search that might lead to an encounter with divine mystery suggested by the Christianity he has sought to rid himself of. But Haze makes little progress because, for Mrs. Flood, he is yet another piece of property to be possessed. In an attempt to escape her fearsome clutches, Haze loses his life. He is a martyr of the "innerdirected" life described in sociologist David Riesman's *The Lonely Crowd*, a seminal book of the fifties.

Mrs. Flood stands out at the end of the novel as a final symbol of the triumph of materialism over the attempts of those with spiritual callings to establish religious revival. Her way of life has indeed "flooded" the world with that way of life in which head, heart, and soul are devoted to possessing things and people (who are themselves treated as things). If O'Connor had discontinued her own spiritual quest at the point in which Haze dies, she might have become, no matter how many subsequent books she might have written, a "one-book" author who proclaims the triumph in the modern world of the materialistic way of life over all spiritual quests. But in her second book, *A Good Man Is Hard to Find*, we see O'Connor's vision of the struggle between violent spiritual quest- ers and materialists trying to manufacture paralyzed worlds for themsel- ves. The struggle of the quester continues in her third book, *The Violent Bear It Away* until, in her fourth and last book, *Everything That Rises Must Converge*, she presented the possibility of meaningful community beyond the stifling, paralyzed communities of modern materialists and the violent assaults of half-mad "prophets" who hurl their rage at those who have denied their existence.

Chapter 6

World Paralysis, World Destruction

In *Wise Blood*, a book many still consider her greatest achievement, Flannery O'Connor follows the inspiration of Nathanael West in presenting people in a modern urban world who are caught up in a crushing alienation, or "aloneness." Attempts to escape alienation through various forms of sexual encounter, through the quest for money and power, and through involvement in the soporific aspects of religion and pseudo-religion are all failures. Those who are aware primarily of O'Connor's critique of a modern world that is rapidly becoming totally urbanized generally read her later work largely in terms of her irony and social satire, both of which can be found shining right through her final stories. But her vision of alienation in the modern city is paralleled by her vision of the young prophet, an individual in some ways much like the artist herself.

The young O'Connor, like her protagonist Haze Motes, was drawn for a time to a form of positivism that viewed the world in terms of scientific and technological ideals. She saw, as Haze did in acting out his self-made materialistic religion without Jesus, that it was possible to proclaim meaning in the modern world by the practice of a pseudo-religion based on the modern world's practical philosophy of automobiles, sex, and rapid movement. But she found, as Joyce did in seeing himself as the young Stephen Dedalus, that one could not so easily escape one's Catholic teaching. Joyce turned to art as a way out of a modern world he despised, but this art, as his *A Portrait of the Artist as a Young Man* reveals, is based primarily on the aesthetics of Thomas Aquinas. O'Connor was, like Joyce, very much concerned with problems of the artist, but she was even more concerned with the role of the Christian prophet in the modern world. In *Wise Blood*, she turned to the problem the Christian must face when he first begins to act on even a few of his assumptions; that problem is the state of his inner life. Haze discovers his inner life contains powerful elements of destruction—hate, lust, arrogance—and by the end of the novel he is meditating on these matters. He does not live long enough to deal extensively with these problems, which, for O'Connor, were connected with the power of evil that Christians have traditionally associated with Satan.

That after *Wise Blood* O'Connor took Satan as a primary topic can be seen in the epigraph to her second book, the short story collection *A Good Man is Hard to Find*. The epigraph, a quotation from St. Cyril of Jerusalem, reads: "The dragon is by the side of the road, watching those who pass. Beware lest he devour you. We go to the Father of Souls, but it is necessary to pass by the dragon." O'Connor never repeated herself in her best fiction, and there would not be another Haze; instead there would be young prophets caught up in destructive and satanic powers which they were only vaguely aware of but which, in their own various ways, they struggled against. Her second book is primarily a vision of the young prophet moving on into the fear of spiritual darkness. Her social scene in *A Good Man is Hard to Find* and a succeeding volume of stories is not so much that of the fragmented urban scene of a Taulkinham as it is of the paralyzed worlds created by those who do not want to move into the future.

In creating various images of social paralysis, O'Connor very much reminds us of Joyce, whose fiction from *Dubliners* through *Ulysses* presents a vision of a society that is paralyzed ("paralysis" is in fact Joyce's term for this condition), a society which casts a pall over its inhabitants, who are described, for instance, in his greatest story, "The Dead," as being empty and isolated, a condition symbolized by falling snow. Unlike Joyce, however, O'Connor was aware of a mood of destructiveness that threatened the paralyzed worlds inhabited by her dead souls. Unlike Haze and those like him who with their automobiles hope to overcome by perpetual flight the effects of paralysis and its accompanying isolation, the active young figures in O'Connor's stories often seek to blow up the paralyzed world they find themselves trapped within. Thus O'Connor, in her second and two succeeding volumes, presented visions of world paralysis and world destruction. But embedded in *A Good Man is Hard to Find* is the seed of a visionary insight into a new world that must follow destruction. In her fourth work, *Everything That Rises Must Converge*, she presented her strongest vision of what this new emerging society might be.

In the first and last stories of *A Good Man Is Hard to Find*, O'Connor presented her profoundest visions of the destruction of paralyzed worlds. In the first story, "A Good Man Is Hard to Find," we find two paralyzed worlds existing side by side. One is the suburban Atlanta world of Bailey and his possessive mother, and the other is the haunted world that is the countryside. By the end of this story both worlds are ravaged by an insane criminal called The Misfit. In the story those individuals representing the two worlds that O'Connor often shows to be in conflict in her fiction—the New South world of Atlanta and the rural Georgia scene—have encountered the dragon by the roadside that tests all souls. This dragon has seized and possessed The Misfit and his small band of fellow murderers. Only The Misfit realizes what force has seized him, but there is nothing he can do to rid himself of satanic possession.

The Misfit is in many ways an extension of Haze Motes. Like Haze, he realizes that he is driven by an inner violence that is destroying both him and others. Like Haze, he has sought to overcome the violence within himself by turning to his inherited Christianity, but, also like Haze, the materialistic outlook he has inherited from his society makes it impossible for him to receive that grace which can free him of his homicidal mania. " 'Jesus was the only One that ever raised the dead,' " The Misfit tells the old lady as he is about to shoot her. She mumbles, " 'Maybe He didn't raise the dead' " (*CS*, 132). The Misfit considers this proposition seriously and replies, " 'I wasn't there so I can't say He didn't. . . . It ain't right I wasn't there because if I had been there I would have known . . . if I had been there I would have known and I wouldn't be like I am now' " (*CS*, 132). The Misfit is thus a materialist and a positivist, even though uneducated; his epistemology will not allow him to accept any event as being true that he has not personally verified. The Church's doctrine that one encounters grace through an act of faith is unknown to him, and, without that grace, he must continue his deadly work of shooting the old lady and her family. If Jesus did raise the dead, The Misfit informs the old lady before he kills her, then " '[I]t's nothing for you to do but throw away everything and follow Him, and if He didn't, then it's nothing for you to do but enjoy the few minutes you got left the best way you can—by killing somebody or burning down his house or doing some other meanness to him' " (*CS*, 132).

That O'Connor means for us to believe The Misfit is possessed by the Devil can be seen primarily in her satirical approach to the psychological terminology used to define The Misfit, as well as by his own acceptance of his cruelty as his one true joy: " 'No pleasure but meanness,' he said and his voice had become almost a snarl" (*CS*, 132). Unable to achieve a new life beyond the violence that possesses him, The

Misfit seeks to destroy the comfortable lives others have created for themselves. Destruction is his answer to the false happiness of paralyzed worlds that individuals and groups have created to shield themselves from any kind of change. In a sense, he is like Christ in seeking to throw off balance the false worlds created by ordinary human beings fleeing God, but, instead of the love which Christ brings to the world, he has only destruction to offer. He says at the end of the story, " 'It's [killing] no real pleasure in life' " (*CS*, 132). He has momentarily glimpsed the old woman as one like his own mother; he even accepts for a second her sudden offer of love before he shoots her. He seems to realize that love is the one good, not violence, but he cannot shake off his chosen role as the destroyer of the paralyzed, loveless worlds of other people. Yet he knows that Jesus, whose grace brings with it love, is also a destroyer of paralyzed worlds. When the old lady at the beginning of her dialogue invokes Jesus' name, The Misfit replies immediately, " 'Jesus thown everything off balance' " (*CS*, 131). Thus, in O'Connor's vision, both Christ and the dragon challenge the worlds that people create for themselves, worlds that seem to cry out for destruction because of their static, loveless nature. Life, The Misfit says, demands continuing change as well as a continuing search for love.

In "The Displaced Person," the final story of her first collection, O'Connor reversed the theme of the destructive outsider by introducing a Christlike figure into a Georgia plantation that is kept firmly in balance by one of those formidable middle-age ladies so often found in O'Connor's work. The lady, Mrs. McIntyre, is a "good Catholic," but, when her priest mentions Christ, her "face assumed a set puritanical expression and she reddened. Christ in the conversation embarrassed her the way sex had her mother" (*CS*, 226). She makes it clear to the priest that the war refugee he brings her as a hired hand on her farm must fit into her own paralyzed world. When Mr. Guizac accepts the farm's black hired hands as his equals, she rejects him and tells the priest, " 'But he doesn't understand how to get on with my niggers and they don't like him. I can't have my niggers run off' " (*CS*, 226). The priest himself is for Mrs. McIntyre only a comfortable part of her loveless world until he proposes that she act charitably toward both Mr. Guizac and her black farmhands. His proposal and the charity of Mr. Guizac himself cause Mrs. McIntyre to withdraw into her own static realm. She is joined in this withdrawal by Mr. Shortley, her white hired hand, and by the blacks themselves who prefer the devil they know to the devil they do not know. The result is the death of Mr. Guizac and the collapse of Mrs. McIntyre's way of life.

Thomas Daniel Young has written that Mr. Guizac is "one of the few characters in the story who resides in grace. He is a devout Catholic."[1] By offering Christ's grace and the love that accompanies it, Mr. Guizac threatens all who are paralyzed. He thus draws from others on the farm diabolical qualities they are unaware of possessing. Mr. Shortley's wife had begun a movement toward diabolism by first hating the displaced person, and her own rage finally killed her. Her internalized anger also ignited in others on the farm their powerful hatred of love itself. Thus Carter Martin has written of the diabolical actions that destroy both Mr. Guizac and the farm: "Mrs. Shortley dies at the height of her anger toward him, but the other three participate in his death, at which their eyes come together in one look that froze them in collusion forever."[2]

In the best stories in *A Good Man Is Hard to Find* those Southerners who cling to some fabricated view of the past become destructive. In one of her most searching critiques of fundamentalist religion, O'Connor, in "The River," revealed the dangers of embracing an emotion-charged ritual without proper preparation. Religion itself, O'Connor seems to have been saying in this story, can be a closed, paralyzed world which devours the outsider, particularly one who comes in innocence seeking a true community, as does the child Bevel. Rejected by his own parents, Bevel is brought by the woman who keeps him to a young prophet who mystifies him with his biblical language. The result is that the child takes him literally when he is offered baptism: " '[Y]ou can lay your pain in that River and get rid of it because that's the River that was made to carry sin' " (*CS*, 165). The boy, without any instruction in the faith, accepts literally the prophet's injunction and drowns himself. His action becomes a final search for the love that is missing in his life. Unable to destroy the paralyzed world in which he finds himself, the boy uses the ritual of baptism to end his own paralyzed life. O'Connor's work often portrays fundamentalist religion as a means of escaping, through some form of violent prophecy, a false social stasis that this kind of religion helps to maintain.

---

[1] Thomas Daniel Young, "Flannery O'Connor's View of the South," *Studies in the Literary Imagination* 20/2 (Fall 1987): 13.

[2] Carter Martin, *The True Country: Themes in the Fiction of Flannery O'Connor* (Nashville: Vanderbilt University Press, 1969) 97.

The instrument of destruction in some of O'Connor's best stories is a confidence man who knows how to appeal to the desires of those who have created a world for themselves. Examples of these stories are "Good Country People" and "The Life You Save May Be Your Own." In both stories, confidence men enter the strangely balanced worlds of two dominating women and attempt to destroy the balance the women have created. In "Good Country People," a Bible Salesman passes himself off to Mrs. Hopewell, the dominating hierarch, as a "good country person" by fitting neatly into her worldview of a hierarchy of Southern gentility which could always offer a kind of patronage to the deserving poor. Mrs. Hopewell has glued her world together with clichés like "Nothing is perfect" and "that is life." For years Mrs. Hopewell had maintained within her paralyzed world an agent of destruction, her daughter Joy, "whose constant outrage had obliterated every expression from her face" (*CS*, 273). Joy, who has a Ph.D. in philosophy, has changed her name to Hulga, partly to attack her mother's shallow optimism. The daughter tries to seduce the young Bible salesman, but instead is seduced and betrayed by the young man. At the beginning of her attempted seduction, when the Bible salesman tells her to say she loves him, she warns the man that she does not use the word "love." In explaining why, she says: " 'I don't have illusions. I'm one of those people who see *through* to nothing' " (*CS*, 287). But, at the end of the story, she herself is psychically demolished by the Bible salesman, who tells her his Christianity is nothing but a pose and that " 'I been believing in nothing ever since I was born!' " (*CS*, 291). When Mrs. Hopewell sees the young man leaving her farm, she still believes in his goodness. But the implication is that her now thoroughly inhibited daughter will accomplish the destruction of the paralyzed world her mother has created.

"Good Country People" has achieved high critical acclaim partly because it effectively treats the corrosive effects of a hidden destructiveness that wells up within the individual and is the result of an attitude of a mind that denies all values. For O'Connor, philosophical positivism, which she once wrote "A" that she was tempted to adopt as her own worldview, contained within it the seeds of a corrosive destructiveness. Positivism for O'Connor was the dominant modern philosophy, one which teaches that nothingness exists behind the material aspects of life. This particular form of modern nihilism, she showed in her stories, can be a weapon used to destroy the comfortable worlds created by hierarchs whose minds are still fixed on an imagined glorious past or on some closed religious system. One of O'Connor's greatest values as a story-teller who was deeply aware of the Southern class system is her ability to show how uneducated people also create in their minds a kind of nihilistic thinking that they often employ to attack paralyzed worlds that they believe have excluded them. "The Artificial Nigger" is probably O'Connor's best story showing an uneducated racist using his poisonous beliefs about blacks to try to annihilate for himself and his grandson the whole city of Atlanta. She once told me that it was in fact her favorite story.

With her usual selection of names for allegorical purposes, in "The Artificial Nigger" O'Connor drew a portrait of a Georgia mountaineer called Mr. Head. This perfectly self-satisfied man has created in his remote mountain country a picture of himself as a perfected hierarch who "had that calm understanding of life that makes him a suitable guide for the young" (CS, 249). Part of his work as guide and teacher is to show his grandson that the city of Atlanta is a place of no value. The boy had been born there and believes that the city possesses at least some value. He continually begs to be taken there. Mr. Head feels that it is his duty to take the boy there so that he may destroy the city totally in the young boy's mind. Mr. Head prepares the boy for this mental destruction by telling him, " 'It'll be full of niggers' " (CS, 252). The boy acts as if he can deal with people of another color, but the old man reminds him that he has never seen a black person: " 'There hasn't been a nigger in this county since we run that one out twelve years ago and that was before you were born' " (CS, 252).

For Mr. Head, blacks are the contaminating element that makes a city a place of no value for any right-thinking person. The story seems to be moving, as the two proceed to Atlanta, toward the usual tragic ending in most of O'Connor's best stories. But "The Artificial Nigger" is a comic story throughout, one in which the hierarch's "head" knowledge is shown to be a delusion. Nelson is like young Enoch Emery in *Wise Blood*. He has that instinctive goodness associated with "wise blood," and this good-ness leads him to those blacks who turn out not to be obstructive ele-ments in a wasteland city but rather a saving principle that reunites him with his grandfather on a human level, one much deeper than that "head" level of existence in which the old man has sought to instruct the child. The question finally raised in the story, and answered by the author, con-cerns the deepest level of human existence. For O'Connor, that level is love in the Christian sense of *agape*, or *caritas*, and this form of love is first manifested to the boy by a group of blacks in the middle of a city that he has been taught to annihilate in his mind. This newfound love also passes over to Mr. Head, who himself is altered for the better in the city he detests.

Stanley Edgar Hyman was the first critic to spell out the way in which O'Connor saw blacks as "images of brotherhood."[3] O'Connor was not, Hyman stated, in "opposition to integration," and, in fact, as Suzanne Paulson has noted, O'Connor, though sometimes accused of racism, believed "The Negro race is above all an icon of suffering." Paulson further said of O'Connor that "sensitivity to suffering forms the very ground of her thought."[4] And one might add, with Hyman, that only through a true fraternity can suffering be overcome. The boy Nelson is briefly included in the fraternity of the Atlanta blacks who befriend him when he becomes separated from Mr. Head, an allegorical figure representing the foolishness of a "head" knowledge separated from true fraternity. Nelson's brief inclusion in black fraternity even touches Mr. Head, enabling him to let go of his "knowledge" in order to receive an action of "grace" that unites him again with the boy. For O'Connor, "grace" is too mysterious a category to formularize; for her, the literary art was a way of dramatizing the possibility of encountering a power, call it what one may, that makes even brief fraternal moments possible. These moments show how a small world, paralyzed by thought, can be destroyed briefly to make way for love. With this brief destruction O'Connor revealed through symbols of true communion, in the Thomas Merton sense of the word, how human beings can once again receive and give love.

If O'Connor had continued to write the way she did in "The Artificial Nigger," she might have lost some of her reputation for hard-nosed satire and found praise for revealing the possibilities of overcoming the dead weight of various forms of prejudice. But she never tried to repeat herself. From the publication of *A Good Man Is Hard to Find* in 1955 to *The Violent Bear It Away* in 1960, O'Connor was struggling with her profoundest and still least understood work. *The Violent Bear It Away* deals with, among other concerns, the theme of a small group of fraternal blacks who, clinging to the old Christianity, help provide a Christian

---

[3]Stanley Edgar Hyman, *Flannery O'Connor* (Minneapolis: University of Minnesota Press, 1966) 42.

[4]Suzanne Morrow Paulson, *Flannery O'Connor: A Study of the Short Fiction* (Boston: Twayne Publishers, 1988) 71.

fraternity to a backwoods prophet named Mason Tarwater. The small group is contrasted with a psychologist and schoolteacher named Rayber, who lives primarily out of his head. But in the central character of the book, Francis Mason Tarwater, O'Connor went beyond all earlier fictional visions to present a figure struggling with an inner satanic voice that drives him toward violence and total egocentrism. Yet at the same time the voice of old Mason, his great uncle, thunders within the boy, telling him to take up the work of a Christian prophet, one who calls human beings to genuine communion. O'Connor in this novel was at last centering on her most significant theme—the possibility of both violence and grace within the same individual. The boy is called to seek a religious vocation, and at the same time he continually rejects this vocation by repeated acts of violence and egocentric escapism. It is a profound theme and one O'Connor dealt with powerfully. Tarwater in many ways resembles Graham Greene's whisky priest in *The Power and the Glory*, a man in flight from God, who at the same time, without always meaning to, is serving God. In a century where profound religious writing is rare and pseudo-religious expression abounds, Greene and O'Connor have given Catholic and other readers two of the great religious novels of the century.

The Violent Bear It Away still awaits a fuller appreciation and analysis it probably cannot receive at this time. It has already received some acute interpretation, but the place of the book in American fiction since 1950 is not yet fully understood. Its value as a work of fiction lies in its vision, as Caroline Gordon immediately pointed out upon its publication. Sheer visionary power is hard to assess, and when it is present there is often a confusion of thought in the reader, if not also in the plot. Although I will briefly seek to place the book in the thematic and stylistic framework of O'Connor's fiction, I must also note that behind the novel's vision lies the deepest confessional writing O'Connor ever did. I emphasize this fact because, as the author realized when she said no biography would be necessary because her outward actions were few, her essential life was lived within the intense scope of her own intellectual, religious, and artistic life. Of course, I disagree with her opinion that a biography is not necessary. As Ezra Pound said of T. S. Eliot, we need to know as much about this particular writer as possible, and the same is true for O'Connor, a writer whose difficulty and importance makes it necessary for us to know as much as we can about her. Like Eliot, and Dostoevski before him, O'Connor as a writer and a person was a strange mixture of intellectual and primitive elements, so strange as to require the profoundest scrutiny.

O'Connor was at once the boy Tarwater, his great uncle, and the teacher Rayber. At the same time she was the visionary and the intellectual artist detached and working behind and through the strange scenes of violence and love so intimately related in the novel. Her understanding of the novel is acutely revealed in letters to Alfred Corn, to myself, and to others. Her second novel haunted her more than any of her works, and will no doubt continue to haunt many of her readers. Like Hawthorne's best fiction, the book contains at once a vision beyond her own or anyone else's at this time in history. Concepts that she struggled with personally are deeply tied up in the book's allegorical framework. Allegory and the mystery of strange vision are the twin powers contained within *The Violent Bear It Away*, making it the author's greatest work in the tradition of the American "romance" as defined by Nathaniel Hawthorne. Thus O'Connor would write John Hawkes: "I think I would admit to writing what Hawthorne called 'romances,' . . . Hawthorne interests me considerably. I feel more of a kinship with him than with any other American" (*HB*, 457). Poe and Hawthorne fascinated O'Connor because they both wrote so deeply about the haunted American mind cut off from other minds—the mind seeking communion with others but failing to find it. And from Joyce she had learned the art of the epiphany and the truth that lies behind Joyce's art, which is that the one who seeks the spiritual realm may momentarily glimpse both spirit and love.

Hawthorne and Poe wrote about questers who were seeking to escape their mental isolation but who fell back into sterility or into that vampirism which Allen Tate believed to be of central concern to Poe. But in O'Connor's work there is always the possibility of escaping sterility and vampirism by discovering love, if only momentarily. She believed that anyone who approached God could find both grace and love. Thus for her a backwoods Protestant like old Mason Tarwater, living in Southern Appalachia and cut off from mainstream America and from the rich heritage of traditional Christianity, best represented for the author by the Catholic Church, could, as she has put it, with his Bible and the aid of the Holy Spirit find the love necessary to make true communion possible. In *The Violent Bear It Away*, O'Connor reconstructs old Tarwater's communal life in terms of his loose association with several blacks and poor whites who form one cadre of what is left, as she sees it, of meaningful Christian community in America. The old man is a self-proclaimed prophet who, as O'Connor wrote me in 1963, discussing his nature, "wasn't all belief without deeds; he was a man who could act" (*HB*, 506). In this letter she was discussing my interpretation of Tarwater as a religious fanatic. One aspect of the humor concerning the old man was indeed his seeming obsession with outdated religious ideas, but for O'Connor he was not a true fanatic, one, that is, whose obsessions lead to his own and other's destruction but was instead, in her words, "what the world calls a fanatic (anyone who believes and acts literally on his belief)" (*HB*, 506-507). The humor of his life is revealed in the occasional absurdity of his attempting to live out beliefs that nearly everyone in the modern world regards as largely meaningless. Yet the novel makes it quite clear that through the mystery of his belief and his receiving of grace, Mason Tarwater in fact escapes the condition of the haunted mind which goes mad because of isolation and obsession. Tarwater is able to love, and through love his life, absurd though it sometimes is, becomes fruitful for others. His "violent" and forceful seizure of the Kingdom of God makes possible fructification in the lives of others.

Tarwater is quite clearly not like the initiatory Christian forebear who sends Haze Motes off to seek a religion separate from Christ. In *Wise Blood* and most of her stories, people fear Christianity because for them it means rage, devil-obsession, and unkindness. Some critics, of course, have seen Mason Tarwater as part of this tradition, which for many seemed to dominate nineteenth-century Christianity—Catholic, Protestant, and other forms. Robert Drake was one of the first critics, however, to see clearly that Mason Tarwater could communicate love to others. The boy Tarwater had received love from him, but he was fleeing love because that love which was early received was connected with his calling to be a prophet. But the atheist Rayber had also, as a child, received love from the old man, love which he could never get rid of, try though he might. Drake thus wrote: "Rayber himself had been baptized by the old man when a boy, had found in him also the only real love he had ever known." Drake pointed out how the love Rayber has for his own idiot child, whom he wishes to categorize in his pseudo-scientific manner as "a mistake of nature," in fact springs from his early association with Mason Tarwater: "But he has thrown off those dark atavistic influences now, he thinks, except that sometimes he is overwhelmed by a blind senseless love for his idiot child."[5]

Atavistic tendencies for Rayber are mainly those engendered by his religious heritage, which he does not understand but which he lumps together with all those ideas of the past that have been discarded by the modern mentality so that science and an education based on it could be the one true religion for the modern world. But, as Hawthorne before O'Connor had shown in characters like Chillingworth in *The Scarlet Letter*, the modern mind cannot find a way out of its isolation because of an obsessive concern with its own complexity and power. In most of her best work O'Connor continually suggested that the conscious intellect alone—in fact, the whole Enlightenment philosophy of salvation through knowledge and intellect—could not bring true community to the industrialized age.

She believed that what is needed, as a letter to Alfred Corn about *The Violent Bear It Away* explains, is the free choice of accepting grace, a choice that usually involves much inner struggle. Neither Rayber nor Tarwater, she wrote, "exhibits a lack of free will. An absence of free will in these characters would mean an absence of conflict in them, whereas they spend all their time fighting within themselves, drive against drive" (*HB*, 489). At the end of this letter, she denied the possibility of her work having a deterministic view, the reason being that she discovered through her writing a continuing growth of both knowledge and mystery: "Mystery isn't something that is gradually evaporating. It grows along with knowledge" (*HB*, 489).

O'Connor was thus clearly not opposed to knowledge of any kind—including science. She was drawn to study the philosophy of positivism and in fact wrote that she preferred Freud to Jung because his work was more anchored in reason than was Jung's. She believed deeply in reason and her closest friend in college, Betty Boyd Love, held a master's degree in mathematics. But she believed that reason and science could not do the work of true religion, whose chief task was to create a living community as opposed to the paralyzed worlds that grew out of the manipulative intellect and from memories of a past glory. Always some new impetus was needed, and this impetus, she believed, must always spring from continuing conscious decisions to open oneself to a spiritual power

---

[5]Robert Drake, *Flannery O'Connor* (Grand Rapids MI: William B. Eerdmans, 1966) 34.

that was so often in her fiction symbolized by the sun. In choosing the sun as symbol, she was following St. Augustine, who used the sun to represent Christ and his glory. But while the chief allegorical forms of this remarkable novel are fascinating, above all else it is necessary to examine the visionary insights contained within *The Violent Bear It Away*.

One of the profoundest visions in *The Violent Bear It Away* is that of the collapsing city—the city of the flight from God that she found most deeply and poetically rendered in Max Picard's book *The Flight From God*. Young Tarwater and his uncle are sitting in an office in a city of 75,000 that very much resembles the Macon, Georgia that the author knew when she was young. But it could also be the Atlanta she visited as a young girl and where she attended high school for a few months. With an almost inherited gift for prophecy, young Tarwater sees into the heart of the city; he sees that essentially it is a place for flight:

> Then he had realized, almost without warning, that this place was evil—the ducked heads, the muttered words, the hastening away. He saw in a burst of light that these people were hastening away from the Lord God Almighty. It was to the city that the prophets came and he was here in the midst of it. He was here enjoying what should have repelled him (*VBIA*, 27).

When he first arrives in the city, Tarwater reacts much in the manner of Enoch Emery in *Wise Blood*: "He wanted to stop and shake hands with each of them and say his name was F. M. Tarwater and that he was here only for the day to accompany his uncle on business at a lawyer's" (*VBIA*, 26). But Tarwater is Enoch and Haze Motes and also a young man who has the Christian gift of prophecy—three people, that is, rolled into one. The boy in him instinctively reaches out to strangers who should be, he believes, part of a living community. Instead they are merely "hulks":

> Several people bumped into him and this contact that should have made an acquaintance for life, made nothing because the hulks moved on with ducked heads and muttered apologies that he would have accepted if they had waited (*VBIA*, 26).

But Tarwater is also Haze wanting to have a place in the city; he enjoys the city more than anything he had known in the country.

Like Haze, Tarwater instinctively and immediately grasps that the flight from God, which is the city's essential nature, can be enjoyable for one who seeks to escape the old decaying and paralyzed provincial communities. For Haze, the automobile and casual sex are the essential ingredients of this new, modern city fleeing God. With a good car, a person never has to stay in a single place for long, and, with casual sex, condoms prevent an individual from becoming tied unwillingly to one place as sexual intercourse in the old rural communities had once done. The city, as Tarwater continues to discover, is filled with drugs, one of them being evangelistic religion, which offers "good feelings" with no price to pay, since no role in a living community is demanded of the participant. The new exploitative evangelism is nothing more than a nostalgia for something that brought a momentary happiness in the remembered preindustrial communities. This remembered happiness is once again conjured up by clever religious charlatans who present it in the form of drugs for weary souls in flight.

Throughout *The Violent Bear It Away*, O'Connor, as in no other work, revealed in a series of visions that the flight carried on within cities is a flight from either dead preindustrial communities or from dying communities that have been kept intact by the paralyzing efforts of a few strong men and women who hypnotize and manipulate those in the community whom they control economically and socially. As in stories like "The Displaced Person," an internal psychic destruction eventually blows up many of these paralyzed communities, and those who survive continue to flee to the cities, where they are continually destroying, in their minds, the old communities.

The city at first seems to offer nothing but flight, yet there is an organization seeking to shape the flight into meaningful order. It is the force of education symbolized by Rayber, who vainly believes an educational system based on the mind alone can create true community. Rayber is obviously not a typical representative of education, but, as one who denied his deepest feelings and who, like Hulga in "Good Country People," prided himself on seeing through to "nothing," he represents for O'Connor the essence of an American form of Cartesianism that she believed dominated education. Thus she described Rayber:

> At his high school he was the expert on testing. All his professional decisions were prefabricated and did not involve his participation. He was not deceived that this was a whole or a full life, he only knew that

it was the way his life had to be lived if it were going to have any dignity at all. He knew he was the stuff of which fanatics and madmen are made and that he had turned his destiny as if with his bare will. He kept himself upright on a very narrow line between madness and emptiness, and when the time came for him to lose his balance, he intended to lurch toward emptiness and fall on the side of his choice (*VBIA*, 114-15).

Rayber's creed consists in a sentence that he continued to pound into young Tarwater when he had him in his control: " 'The great dignity of man . . . is his ability to say I am born once and no more' " (*VBIA*, 172). Man can achieve dignity, Rayber believes, only if he relinquishes all religious ideas and accepts the eighteenth-century Enlightenment doctrine of progress, the belief that only through social and material engineering can true community come into being. As a standard bearer of the doctrine of progress, Rayber accepts his life as that of a modern hero: "He recognized that in silent ways he lived an heroic life. The boy would go either his way or old Tarwater's and he was determined to save him for the better course" (*VBIA*, 115).

O'Connor was dissatisfied with her characterization of Rayber and said as much to me and to others, Richard Gilman among them. Yet I think the character fits perfectly into the book's basic vision. Her dissatisfaction with the character was based, I believe, on her own failure to understand the kind of surrealistic, absurdist work of art that she had created. Her dissatisfaction was increased by the immediate failure of others from whom she sought understanding. My own reply to the copy of the book she sent me upon publication was completely inadequate, but then I had never encountered a novel remotely like this one. While understanding the allegorical insights, I failed to grasp the book's vision, and I know of no one else at the time who did. Certainly the reviewers of the book failed to see what *The Violent Bear It Away* was all about.

The Violent Bear It Away is, I can now see, a vision of the disappearance of a South that was, like the preindustrialized world everywhere, based on institutions of religion in association with institutions of education, of family, of government, of hierarchies of social relationship. Where these institutions exist at all in the novel, they have become paralyzed. The result is flight from paralysis and a search for individual happiness—a joy belonging to oneself alone and achieved for most people through speed, sex, and showy spectacles like religious extravaganzas, military shows, circuses of various types, athletic contests, and electronic entertainment. Only one institution in the book seems to offer people as a whole the opportunity to work together for the good life; this is the institution of education. But in Rayber, O'Connor has presented a figure who sums up what education conceived along Cartesian lines eventually becomes: a dull, stoic attachment to "testing." At the time she wrote her second novel, the test was not seen as the centerpiece of the educational process, but in making Rayber an expert in educational testing she was anticipating the contemporary movement of educational priority toward objective testing and away from the inner life of the individual. O'Connor also anticipated the demands of modern society in general for an educational establishment at the secondary level that would take over all the functions once reserved for family, religion, and government. But even Rayber, who is a cold fanatic, knows that he has nothing emotional to offer the children he seeks to guide. He gradually comes to see that it is emotional response that his students seek more than anything else, yet he cannot provide that response even though his own love for his idiot child is always welling up from profound depths within himself.

The allegorical meaning of *The Violent Bear It Away* has often been explored and will continue to be explained, outlined, and debated. But it is the strangeness and power of the book's vision that has not yet been absorbed deeply by even the best readers of O'Connor. "Why did she see through a glass darkly, rather than face to face?" Hyman asked. He replied to his own question, "There are many answers, and no certain answer."[6] The most obvious answer is that all visionary writing, particularly in the area of religion, contains a "dark" element. Gordon's term "Blakean" comes nearest to describing that kind of authentic religious vision that is contained in *The Violent Bear It Away*, more than in any of her works. Vision is not vision if the author understands fully what she is writing. My own awareness of O'Connor as a person led me gradually to believe that she was, up to the time of her death, continuing to develop her literary vision, one which often haunted her and which she struggled to express without always being able to understand or explain it.

O'Connor's visionary power was the deepest quality in her artistic creativity, and our loss of it is a literary and religious tragedy for many. The power of this vision is experienced by the reader in terms of language and more explorations of this visionary language of the kind

---

[6]Hyman, *Flannery O'Connor*, 8.

Edward Kessler has given is very much needed. In his *Flannery O'Connor and the Language of Apocalypse*, Kessler wrote:

> Flannery O'Connor creates her visionary poetics, uniting her with those who do not name but *see* the infinite in everything. Before her reader can be "turned" toward the absolute, he must engage with the metaphoric process because the thing itself, whether word or image, remains inert until acted upon.[7]

What Kessler wrote is true, but is also true that O'Connor's particular kind of visionary experience, which was religious both in the Dantean and the Blakean sense, is so strange to many modern readers that before these readers can be urged to make a serious attempt to "engage with the metaphoric process," they must be shown the relevance to their own lives of the larger issues contained within literary and religious vision. I had various discussions with O'Connor about this issue: the teaching of readers who were visionary illiterates—and some of the results can be found in four of my published articles on the subject.[8] What I propose, in conclusion, is to discuss some of these larger issues both in connection with *The Violent Bear It Away* and, in the next and concluding chapter, with her last work, *Everything That Rises Must Converge*.

The chief elements of O'Connor's vision in *The Violent Bear It Away* are four characters: Old Tarwater, Rayber, Young Tarwater, and the child Bishop. O'Connor made it clear in several places that she was fully on old Tarwater's side as a Christian hierarch who teaches and baptizes the young. Old Tarwater is a man who can act, one who is "violent," or forceful, as the word "violent" from scripture can also be translated, in seizing and bearing away for himself the Kingdom of God, which is not in heaven alone or a state that will one day appear but is to be found everywhere by those who search for it. Tarwater is one who has searched, found, and borne away, for himself and others, the Kingdom. O'Connor's deepest visionary insight can be found in her characterization of old Tarwater in terms of his suffering, his prophetic insights and

---

[7]Edward Kessler, *Flannery O'Connor and the Language of the Apocalypse* (Princeton NJ: Princeton University Press, 1986) 84.

[8]See the following articles: "Flannery O'Connor's View of God and Man," *Studies in Short Fiction* 1 (Fall 1964): 200-206; "Flannery's South: Don Quixote Rides Again," *Flannery O'Connor Bulletin* 1 (Fall 1972): 39-46; "Flannery O'Connor, the New Criticism, and Deconstruction," *Southern Review* 23/2 (Spring 1987): 271-81.

actions, his alienation in an unbelieving world, and in his fraternal association with several blacks, including the enigmatic Buford Munson and a black prophetess, who make up a cadre of believing Christians. As for Rayber, O'Connor's portrait extends far beyond her allegorical portrait of him as a modern gnostic, to use a term that is at the center of Eric Voegelin's philosophy, which influenced her to a certain extent. Rayber is haunted by his love for his child, a love he cannot understand or rid himself of. As a Cartesian and a son of the eighteenth-century Enlightenment, he is at war within himself—split between his unrepressable love and his desire to conform his life and other lives to a system of knowledge that has no explanation or place for love. O'Connor's visionary rendering of his character is filled with pity at his blind suffering as well as with a sense of stern prophecy, a prophecy that does not condemn but instead warns of the danger of his failing mission.

O'Connor's deepest and most difficult visionary insight is to be found in her creation of young Tarwater and the idiot child. No one in contemporary literature has written so mystically and so touchingly about children living in a society that denies their deepest existence. The idiocy of the child for O'Connor was but one of many signs of the child's relationship to divinity. Writing of young Tarwater, O'Connor drew on her deepest powers of vision to probe the depth of a soul that is trying to escape a prophetic mission that springs from a belief in a Christ that he, like Haze Motes, cannot rid himself of, try as he may. The mystery of a religious power that is hated, feared, fled from in desperation is the subject of this aspect of O'Connor's vision. Tarwater becomes everyman. Divided between the tar of death and the water of life, Tarwater seeks at once to throw off the life power within himself in order to enjoy his own desires and pleasures and at the same time finds that he cannot free himself of an inherited awareness of the springs of divine existence.

Tarwater is also seen in connection with the mystery of evil, which is most immediate for him in the voice of the devil urging him to deny a belief in the divine and cling to a belief in the ego and its desires. The two forces in Tarwater meet in one of the most mysterious actions in modern literature, when the divinely inspired young man baptizes the child and the same diabolically inspired person murders the child. This action leads to an encounter with a devil actually in the flesh, the renouncing of this devil by Tarwater, and the acceptance of a prophetic mission. In her murder-baptism scene, O'Connor revealed a profound aspect of modernity—the destruction of an old world, including its religion—and the summoning through the ritual of water purification—the world's oldest ritual—the new life of a new age that would link humankind to God in true community.

It now remains to consider O'Connor's vision of the growth of a new communal association of humanity, based as they were on visions similar to those of Teilhard de Chardin and Thomas Merton, two modern Catholic thinkers who influenced O'Connor and whom she often resembled in her writing and thought. From her struggle with individuals like Tarwater and Haze Motes, both caught up in Protestant visions of hell and individual "salvation," she moved on to consider the possibility of religious vision beyond both a Thomistic Catholicism and a Calvinistic Protestantism.

Chapter 7

The Renewal of Community

In Flannery O'Connor's fourth volume, *Everything That Rises Must Converge*, an apocalyptic vision of true community begins to emerge. This book, like her three earlier works of fiction, continues the theme of the violent destruction of old, paralyzed worlds. Her awareness of the shadow quality of modern violence does not diminish nor does her sense of the mystery of evil; yet, in stories like "Revelation" and "The Enduring Chill," there is a new sense of the renewing of a life grounded not in hate but rather in a sympathy achieved through a renewal of community.

Joyce Carol Oates has, more strikingly than any other critic, gone to the heart of O'Connor's apocalyptic vision. For Oates the most powerful of O'Connor's visions of renewed community is to be found in her story "Revelation," a work in which Mrs. Turpin, a yeoman farmer who, with her husband, has enough of the goods of life to be physically comfortable while still lacking a true sympathy for those around her, particularly those blacks and poor whites who, she believes, deserve their low positions in life because of some imagined failure of virtue. But her vision of the collapse of the paralyzed world, which she has partly inherited and partly created in her own mind, leads not, as in so many other O'Connor stories, to death but rather to a vision of a new communal life that she can enter at any time she chooses. The suffering she experiences becomes purgatorial when she seeks through vision a way beyond desolation. Of the story "Revelation," Oates stated: "This is the most powerful of O'Connor's revelations, because it questions the very assumptions of the ethical life."[1] In her vision Mrs. Turpin sees a group of pilgrims representing the various social classes of the South. These pilgrims are moving toward heaven as a communal group rather than as a collection of isolated individuals who detest and fear each other. Mrs. Turpin is surprised to see that her own virtues have been burned away. Continuing her discussion of the story, Oates wrote: "It is not simply our 'virtues' that

---

[1]Joyce Carol Oates, "The Visionary Art of Flannery O'Connor," in *Flannery O'Connor*, ed. Bloom, 52.

will be burned away but our rational faculties as well, and perhaps even the illusion of our separate, isolated egos."[2]

Like others who have written about O'Connor's vision of community, Oates pointed to the formative influence of Teilhard de Chardin: "Like Teilhard, O'Connor is ready to acquiesce to the evolution of a form of higher consciousness that may be forcing itself into the world *at our expense*."[3] In O'Connor's last book there is a stronger sense than in any earlier work of the painful renunciation of the old, static worlds that have been substituted for community. The expense Oates wrote of is the agony of those who are caught up in the collapse of long-prized social structures. But Oates, like O'Connor, is a woman who also writes of violence and renewal in modern life. Oates has written that the emergence of new community is inevitable: "Man cannot remain what he is; he cannot exist without being transformed. We are confronted, says Teilhard, with two directions and only two: one upward and the other downward."[4] Yet for O'Connor, Teilhard was only an inspiration, not a revered master like Aquinas. His prophecy and a few of his apocalyptic words moved her, the most notable words being, "Everything that rises must converge."

My own arguments with Flannery concerning Teilhard were convoluted and, given my first belief that she held only to a traditional Catholic orthodoxy, partially mistaken. As I knew her to be a reader and believer in St. Thomas Aquinas, at first I saw only the insider aspects of her viewpoint as opposed to her outsider viewpoint in certain matters of religion. A typical insider comment about Catholicism and St. Thomas, for instance, was made to "A" in 1955: "I wish St. Thomas were handy to consult about the fascist business" (*HB*, 97). On 30 November 1959 she wrote that "I haven't read Pére Teilhard yet so I don't know whether I agree with you or not on *The Phenomenon of Man*" (*HB*, 361). But on 9 April 1960 she wrote to me with great assurance about Teilhard's thought, correcting what she believed was my mistaken belief that his views in *The Phenomenon of Man* were unorthodox. I had merely raised the question about his orthodoxy, believing it would please her that I was gradually beginning to understand some of the finer points concerning that orthodoxy. In 1959 and 1960 she saw me as a "Protestant" and inaccurately describes me as such in several letters. On Teilhard she wrote

---

[2]Ibid.
[3]Ibid.
[4]Ibid.

to me that *The Phenomenon of Man* is not about animals but about development. She stated on 6 April 1960: "The man is a scientist, writing as one" (*HB*, 388). In the same paragraph she contradicts her description of Teilhard as being no more than a scientist: "This is a scientific age and Teilhard's direction is to face it toward Christ" (*HB*, 388). Then in correcting my reading of Teilhard, she remonstrated, "Talk about this man after you know something about him" (*HB*, 388).

I still hold to my view that there is no way to square Teilhard with Aquinas, and I gather that strictly orthodox Catholics do not try to. Liberal Catholics, particularly in America, often take Teilhard to be a kind of Christian prophet, but usually these liberals reject O'Connor's work as too Jansenist, that is, as fiction that places far too much emphasis on sin and grace to be truly liberal in viewpoint. I think the popular and traditional Catholic writer Malachi Martin summed up much of what many orthodox Catholics still have against Teilhard. For Martin, Teilhard "successfully in terms of logic made Jesus only a man" and, further, "He made the human reality we see and touch and measure and use throughout our universe into the truth of all our being and into the truth of all the universe."[5] Martin continued, "that reality [Teilhard's] is not the truth, but the material and physical setting of the truth."[6] I make much of O'Connor's view of Teilhard to suggest, once again, that here was another example of that side of her role as artist and thinker that I call the outsider aspect. She was, in a sense, often at work subverting many of her insider traditional views for her own prophetic and artistic purposes, which she herself did not always understand.

Above all else, O'Connor found in Teilhard certain phrases and ideas that she needed to reveal in her fiction her own apocalyptic vision of a new and better period in world history. In a letter to Roslyn Barnes on 29 March 1961, she clearly stated how this process worked for her in connection with Teilhard and with, for that matter, certain other thinkers whose ideas affected her work. She writes of having sold to *New World Writing* the story "Everything That Rises Must Converge." Then she stated that the idea of rising and converging "is a physical proposition that I found in Pére Teilhard and am applying to a certain situation in the Southern states & indeed in all the world" (*HB*, 438). The certain situation she spoke of is racism, a Southern and a worldwide problem that is

---

[5]Malachi Martin, *Jesus Now* (New York: Popular Library, 1973) 302.
[6]Ibid.

part of the even larger problem involving the pride of certain groups which regard themselves as superior to other groups. In her work she showed these groups believing that they have the right to dominate and manipulate other groups considered to be of less importance than themselves. Thus the sexism, false nationalism, classism, and other destructive attitudes so well documented by Suzanne Paulson are all part, as O'Connor's work reveals, of the attitude of a proud individualism which prevents humanity from rising and converging. Converging for both Teilhard and O'Connor meant the growth of sympathy through the acceptance of the essential equality of all human beings.

O'Connor would use the title of the story "Everything That Rises Must Converge" for the title of her last collection, which was published a year after her death. Even near death she was working hard to complete the stories for this book, and there can be no doubt that she believed deeply in her dominating theme that individuals can and even now are moving beyond obsession with their own individualism and group identities in order to achieve a true social convergence. And yet the title story reveals only a small insight concerning convergence. Only at the end of the story does one of the characters have an epiphany that reveals to him that both he and his mother have been wrong in clinging to their own rigid ways of thinking. But the mother's death makes it impossible for her to change her ways and one wonders if the son, even as he suddenly sees the essential unity that binds them to each other and to all people, is capable of change. As I have already suggested, "Revelation" and "The Enduring Chill" are the chief stories in the volume which reveal the possibility of a continuing spiritual elevation leading to convergence in new community. This convergence can only follow a "rising" that is essentially a growth of the visionary insight that all people are united already in their inmost nature. The intellectual insight of essential unity, for O'Connor, is of itself not enough; what is needed is the kind of vision that convinces the total self and, for the author, this vision follows the suffering that results from an encounter with destructive forces.

In her linking of the destructive element in human affairs to the rising to a newfound human sympathy, O'Connor clearly grew beyond Teilhard, whose orthodoxy as a Christian prophet is rightly challenged by Catholic apologists like Malachi Martin as well as by the Vatican itself, which in its conservatism has never been comfortable with Teilhard's thought as opposed to his empirical scientific work. Unlike O'Connor, Teilhard failed to take into account the mystery of suffering and of evil in the evolution of humanity to higher existence. Like Sophocles, Dante, and Shakespeare, O'Connor revealed the growth of individuals through the acceptance of suffering, which often springs from the work of the diabolical principle. For her friend John Hawkes, the novelist who sometimes read her work and suggested changes in it, O'Connor was an author involved in some ways in the diabolical. His well-known essay, "Flannery O'Connor's Devil," which appeared in 1962 in the same issue of the *Sewanee Review* as her story "The Lame Shall Enter First," represents a kind of countermovement to those many critics who interpret O'Connor from an orthodox Catholic viewpoint. Hawkes in this essay wrote that "the creative process threatens the Holy throughout Flannery O'Connor's fiction by generating a paradoxical fusion of improbability and passion out of the Protestant 'do-it-yourself' evangelism of the South."[7] Thus, he continued, in O'Connor's work "the creative process transforms the writer's objective Catholic knowledge of the devil into an authorial attitude in some measure diabolical."[8] Hawkes stated that "There is no security, no answer, to be found in either of these horrifying and brightly imagined worlds."[9] For Hawkes, as for Harold Bloom, the whole of O'Connor's fictional world has been seized by the power of that force Jung called the shadow. For Bloom, O'Connor's fictional world, like those created by William Faulkner and T. S. Eliot, is "the American version of the cosmological emptiness that the ancient Gnostics called Nekenoma, a sphere ruled by a demiurge who has usurped the alien God and who has exiled God out of history and beyond the reach of our prayers."[10]

Readings of O'Connor like those offered by Hawkes and Bloom are, for most students of her religious vision, much too sweeping. Yet both critics do point to certain valid aspects of O'Connor's vision, particularly her awareness of diabolical forces within everyone; but, for her, these forces were always accompanied, even in homicidal criminals like The Misfit, by some aspect of God's grace. Her visionary understanding of the human being is that he or she is always caught up in a continuing struggle between creative and destructive forces. But even the most destructive individuals are, at least occasionally, seeking a way beyond

---

[7]John Hawkes, "Flannery O'Connor's Devil," in *Flannery O'Connor*, ed. Bloom, 13.
[8]Ibid.
[9]Ibid, 12.
[10]Harold Bloom, "Introduction," in *Flannery O'Connor*, ed. Bloom, 4.

their own destructiveness to what students of modern religious visionaries like Thomas Merton have called the true self of humanity, which exists at a deeper level than any relatively surface traits, even those of race, gender, class, or nation. I think there is enough evidence in O'Connor's letters and in her profoundest fiction to show that she did have much in common with a visionary like Merton. In fact an understanding of Merton may well be necessary for entering into the O'Connor religious vision. But before examining her similarity to Merton, it is necessary to look at the role of the destructive element in her apocalypse.

Even Joyce Carol Oates has failed to see the role of the Devil in O'Connor's apocalypse. The very word *apocalypse*—Greek simply for the disclosure of that which was hidden or closed—points in Christianity and other religions to an initial challenge by destructive forces followed by acts of faith and invocation leading to an announcement of the sacred. Nowhere in her stories is this better seen than in "Revelation." Mrs. Turpin by the very destructiveness of her prejudiced vision of social and racial groups as unequal in their basic nature calls forth the profound denunciation of a young woman who snarls at her: " 'Go back to hell where you came from, you old wart hog' " (*CS*, 500). The very viciousness of the rebuke drives Mrs. Turpin to consider her own inner hatreds. Bad though she is, she must ask herself if she is really a creature from hell. Only one answer will satisfy her, one from the realm of the sacred. O'Connor believed that any person's prayer, made with contrition and a sincere desire to receive an answer, would be met with a sacred encounter. What Mrs. Turpin receives is a vision revealing her true nature. This oft quoted visionary passage at the end of "Revelation"—the peak, I believe, of O'Connor's visionary art—reveals to Mrs. Turpin that she is one of a group of people moving toward heaven. The fact that she is traveling in company with, among others, the blacks and poor whites who she believed were fundamentally different from and inferior to her is a statement to her that the self within all human beings is the same.

Mrs. Turpin has received in visionary terms the doctrine imparted, for instance, by St. Paul to the Athenians at Mars Hill, which was that God "hath made of one blood all nations of men." The highest calling of "all nations of men," St. Paul tells his Athenian listeners, is "that they should seek the Lord." Finally, he tells them that their own poets have also delivered to them this teaching. The relationship between O'Connor and the Greek tragic poet Sophocles is made, fittingly, by Thomas Merton himself in *Jubilee*. Merton, in assessing her work, found O'Connor to be essentially more like Sophocles than like Hemingway or Katherine Anne Porter. The reason is that in O'Connor we see how, through suffering and evil, human beings learn to realize the essential human core in themselves and others. The Greek playwrights continually point in their works to the role of suffering in bringing forth those visions that lead to a wisdom grounded in a pity and fear that announce the essential human self to all people.

A former associate of Merton's at the Abbey of Gethsemani, John Finley, in a study of Merton's own vision, made many points about his friend that apply to O'Connor. The sense of emptiness in O'Connor's fictional world that is noted by Bloom and other critics was in fact a necessary prelude for a beseeching of the divine ground. Thus Finley wrote: "The emptiness, the dread, and the darkness of prayer are echoes of this call from God. . . . our sinfulness, and our pettiness are invitations, graces, and calls, not to despair but to a total abandonment and emptying of ourselves into the power and presence of God."[11] The burden of Finley's book is to show how Merton's quest for God lead to the destruction of a false self and the emergence, through vision, of the one true self that is at the center of all human existence. The language of vision for both Merton and O'Connor is essentially that of communion. The visionary symbol, Finley said of Merton's definition of communication, "is not to convey information but to open unknown depths of awareness enabling the disciple to come upon the center of his own existence."[12] Merton himself, as Finley has shown, called this center the human being's "ontological roots in a mystery of being that transcends his individual ego."

O'Connor in her fiction expanded the meaning of self to show the individual being united with the spark of God within his or her soul. This act of union generally springs from an awareness of the work of Satan within one's own psyche and the psyche of others. For instance, in the first story of *Everything That Rises Must Converge*, which for most readers seems to offer little of that spiritual rise toward convergence that the title suggests, Julian's final vision at once brings him face to face with a diabolical side of himself. But in his confrontation with this aspect of himself, there is a moment of purgatorial suffering and with it the

---

[11]James Finley, *Merton's Palace of Nowhere: A Search for God through Awareness of the True Self* (Notre Dame IL: Ave Maria Press, 1983) 147.

[12]Ibid., 123.

vision that he has always loved his mother and that their love is the essential fact of their shared existence. When O'Connor shows one of her characters momentarily encountering his or her true self, she shows that encounter as always being involved with the discovery of a larger body of human beings, all of whom are called to move together as a pilgrim city, the one true City of God that the author believed existed behind and through all the secular cities of the world.

From *Wise Blood* through the last story of *Everything That Rises Must Converge* O'Connor's secular city, which by and large must deny the one pilgrim city, is not a single entity but rather a collection of small warring worlds headed downward toward death. Frederick Asals stated in clarifying terms the nature of these enclosed worlds that contain most of O'Connor's protagonists:

> The protagonists of O'Connor's stories all cling to a narrow sense of order, whether the balanced social order of her many matrons or the desiccated rationalism of the intellectuals, for it allows them to feel safe from the terrors that they sense hovering menacingly both within and without.[13]

Asals described the greatest of these terrors as death, but in a story like "Everything That Rises Must Converge," when death finally comes for Julian's mother, the young man is cast out of his ordered Cartesian world of a masculine, overly intellectualized liberalism and discovers first the love that flows from this true self and then next discovers, in the concluding words of the story, "his entry into the world of guilt and sorrow" (*CS*, 420). By acknowledging his guilt and accepting his sorrow, he can, through the willing acceptance of a purgatorial suffering, begin the ascent with all other pilgrims moving toward a convergence with the love of God, the love that binds individuals to each other.

Before Julian experiences the revelation of his love for his mother— that love which opens the door to his authentic existence along with his necessary acceptance of guilt for causing her death—he has sought with his liberal utopianism to destroy his mother's racist, traditional world of that dying pre-civil-rights South which she clings to. He shouts at his mother: " 'You needn't act as if the world had come to an end. . . . From

---

[13]Frederick Asals, *Flannery O'Connor: The Imagination of Extremity* (Athens: University of Georgia Press, 1982) 254.

now on you've got to live in a new world and face a few realities for a change' " (*CS*, 419). The irony of this statement is that Julian's own "narrow sense of order," to use Asal's term, is devoid of the basic reality of love. He calls on his mother to live in a new world, but the only world for O'Connor that is free from destruction is the ever renewing world of the pilgrim city leading toward a full realization of the divine order. The old secular worlds are continually being destroyed because they at last become stifling, and some of those who live in them find eventually that they are moved to destroy these false social orders which deny the reality of true community.

In "The Lame Shall Enter First," O'Connor wrote about a man's visionary encounter with a devil he has invited into his own arid world erected solely on education, science, and good deeds. As various critics have noted, this novella, as it was called when it first appeared in *The Sewanee Review* in 1962, is in some ways a continuation of *The Violent Bear It Away*. The teacher Rayber has become Sheppard, a city recreational director, and the young prophet Tarwater has become a juvenile delinquent and religious fanatic called Johnson. Like Tarwater, Johnson cannot escape his role as religious prophet nor can he rid himself of his own personal devil. By the end of the story the reformer Sheppard is overcome by the prophetic vision of Johnson, who tells his would-be mentor that he is in the hands of the Devil. Johnson himself knows that in time he will, by acts of contrition, accept the rising purgatorial pilgrimage. Yet Sheppard is not destroyed by his personal devil, though the arid world that he inhabits causes the death of his son Norton. This death leads to an awareness of his love for the child and this awareness, as in Julian's case, opens the door to the possibility of the acceptance of purgatory: "His heart constricted with a repulsion for himself so clear and intense that he gasped for breath" (*CS*, 481). What Sheppard sees in the brief vision that brings to him the reality of his true self is that what he considered to be good deeds were in fact an attempt to create a world for himself in which he could worship a false narcissistic self that he took to be the person he really was: "He had stuffed his own emptiness with good works like a glutton. He had ignored his own child to feed his vision of himself. He saw the clear-eyed Devil, the sounder of hearts, leering at him from the eyes of Johnson. His image of himself shrivelled until everything was black before him" (*CS*, 481). Here is possibly O'Connor's most powerful statement of the first movement of apocalypse. This movement is that of the Devil's shattering of the old, false worlds with their false self-images. O'Connor's visionary language here, as usual, is simple and idiomatic. It is a language far removed from the mystical imagery of St. John the Divine, and yet it is apocalyptic in a way similar to St. John's revelation. The same may be said for the language of O'Connor's vision of the second movement of apocalypse, the movement in "Revelation" away from the Devil toward God. Most careful readers, I think, would agree that Mrs. Turpin's vision of the pilgrim's movement toward heaven is O'Connor's best depiction of a rising that must lead to convergence.

For O'Connor, the movement upward of her protagonists is essentially purgatorial. Their encounter with the diabolical helps them to release their hold on the false images of self so that they can begin the slow rise of their psyches toward a full realization of the true self. In "The Enduring Chill," Asbury, the protagonist, has constructed a false self for himself through the worship of Art: "He had failed his god, Art, but he had been a faithful servant and Art was sending him Death. He had seen this from the first with a kind of mystical clarity" (*CS*, 373). Those caught in the web of a false self are supported by pseudo-visions which provide comfortable assurances that the dictates of the false self are always true. Asbury's visiter, Mary George, sees the falsity of Asbury's life. She tells her mother, " 'You've got to face the facts: Asbury can't write so he gets sick. He's going to be an invalid instead of an artist' " (*CS*, 373). What he needs, according to her, is " 'Two or three shock treatments' " (*CS*, 373).

Asbury's initial shock treatment is provided by a priest that his mother summons to what the young man believes is his deathbed. Although he is not a Roman Catholic, Asbury believes that if a Jesuit is sent for he "would talk to a man of culture before he died—even in this desert! Furthermore, nothing would irritate his mother so much" (*CS*, 371). When the priest arrives, he immediately begins his essential work of inquiring into the readiness of the young man's soul for death, which, he says, may come for anybody at any time. With his false self intact, Asbury tries to talk about James Joyce but the priest has never heard of Joyce. Instead, the Jesuit asks Asbury if he prays. Only through prayer, he says, can the soul hope to rise. O'Connor made it clear that the act of rising, as she defined it in her last volume, is in fact the purgatorial ascent of the soul. When the priest meets Asbury, he clearly announces, " 'I'm Father Finn—from Purrgatory.' " (*CS*, 375). The priest explains that his chief work at the time of a soul's crisis is to announce the need to begin the purgatorial ascent. Regular prayer is necessary for the ascent because only through prayer can the soul experience the descent of the Holy Spirit, that power bringing with it the grace that makes the growth of love possible. Only through love is the true self, as well as true community, gradually encountered.

Father Finn tells Asbury that " 'The Holy Ghost will not come until you see yourself as you are—a lazy ignorant conceited youth!' " (*CS,* 377). Asbury responds by opening his eyes to the false self he has created and believed in. The result is that he can begin a new purgatorial existence, announced at the end of the story by a "blinding red-gold sun," which moves from "under a purple cloud." Following St. Augustine's use of the sun as a symbol for Christ, O'Connor in this as well as other stories announces the true King in a "purple cloud," summoning all those who, like Asbury and Mrs. Turpin, would enter the pilgrim community. By accepting purgatorial ascent, Asbury at the end of the story encounters the descending Spirit, which will keep him alive in purgatorial suffering for years to come:

> He saw that for the rest of his days, frail, racked, but enduring, he would live in the face of a purifying terror. A feeble cry, a last impossible protest escaped him. But the Holy Ghost, emblazoned in ice instead of fire, continued, implacable, to descend (*CS,* 382).

"The Enduring Chill" is probably the most theologically explicit of all of O'Connor's stories, yet it lacks the imaginative power of certain other stories in both her collections. Yet "The Enduring Chill" and several other stories in *Everything That Rises Must Converge* clearly measure up to what Lewis P. Simpson has said is the new direction that she and Walker Percy have taken Southern fiction. Flannery O'Connor, he wrote, "has refocused the Southern fictional imperative. Rejecting the mode of remembering—of unworldly assimilating history to memory— she has embraced the mode of revelation."[14] Simpson defined the basis of O'Connor's "mode of revelation" in this manner: "Prophesying the irresistibility of God's grace in the life of the individual, her stories

---

[14]Lewis P. Simpson, *The Brazen Face of History* (Baton Rouge: Louisiana State University Press, 1980) 246.

follow a compelling aesthetic of revelation."[15] And then he correctly summed up stories like "The Enduring Chill" and "Revelation": "Her vision is directed toward timeless order and the beatitude of the soul."[16] In her two novels and in certain stories, beginning with "The Artificial Nigger," O'Connor helped to make us aware that behind human suffering exists a timeless order that calls for a purgatorial "rising." And yet in other stories it is quite correct to draw the conclusion that the divine order and beatitude are blotted out of the minds of her characters by a diabolical force seemingly too strong for them.

O'Connor challenged John Hawkes's interpretation of her work as having in it the power of the Devil. "You haven't convinced me," she wrote Hawkes on 28 November 1961 concerning his article "Flannery O'Connor's Devil," that "I write with the Devil's will or belong in the romantic tradition" (*HB*, 456). Hawkes, of course, overstated the extent of the role of the Devil in O'Connor's writing, though one of his statements has at least a measure of truth in it: "[T]hroughout this fiction, the creative process transforms the writer's objective Catholic knowledge of the devil into an authorial attitude in some measure diabolical."[17] I do not believe that the writer's "objective knowledge of Catholicism" was by any means transformed by her authorial attitude. Like Bernanos and Mauriac, whose influence is often strong in her work, she viewed the Devil, in Catholic terms, as a tempting spirit limited by God in his activities. I wrote as much, with her full approval, about "The Lame Shall Enter First" and some other of her works: "Miss O'Connor's orthodoxy did not allow her to fall into the Manichaean heresy that the Devil is a separate power at war with God. For her, as for the Church, evil is the absence of good, and man is saved from the Devil residing within the human heart by the submission of the whole self to God."[18] Yet I see, long after writing this passage, that O'Connor was deeply influenced by Poe and Hawthorne, whose romantic influence she seems to deny in her letter to Hawkes. Because of her close association with Allen Tate and Caroline Gordon, she was inevitably a part of the modern symbolist movement. Anna Balakian has connected the beginnings of symbolism in Baudelaire

---

[15]Ibid., 246.

[16]Ibid., 248.

[17]Hawkes, "Flannery O'Connor's Devil," 13.

[18]Ted R. Spivey, "Flannery O'Connor: Georgia's Theological Storyteller," in *The Humanities in the Contemporary South*, 26.

with the romanticism of Poe: "This association of the angelic and the diabolical was something that Baudelaire observed in Edgar Allan Poe. . . . After Baudelaire this obsession with the abyss will become one of the chief characteristics of the mental attitude of what was called 'decadent.' "[19] As I have earlier suggested, O'Connor was deeply immersed in texts. As one deeply involved in various intertextual struggles, she inevitably took into herself many of the attitudes and powers of those romantics and symbolists she deeply admired. Yet there is also evidence that O'Connor was, as an individual as well as a writer, struggling with a sense of the destructive in human existence. Indeed, all authors like O'Connor who possess a strong sense of good and evil must inevitably have bouts with powers that seem diabolical.

Louise Hardeman Abbot, in her memoir of O'Connor, presented an individual who possessed a powerful awareness of both good and evil. In a conversation with Abbot, O'Connor stated: " 'I believe in a good deal of Hell's fire on this earth and if I thought of myself in such a way for a minute I'd consign myself to it promptly.' "[20] She was speaking of a remark Abbot had made about her being a "famous person." The remark was followed by O'Connor's scowl, of which Abbot wrote: "It was a splendid scowl and it intimidated me greatly."[21] Various memoirs of O'Connor reveal her formidable quality, as does Abbot's, but Abbot also reported "something terrifying in Flannery." Abbot noted that some people believed that this terrifying quality was related to "coldness or cruelty," but for Abbot it was partly "the terror of encountering humility and charity of such depth and such a fierce and faithful holding on to the truth."[22]

I make much of the strange feelings that the presence of O'Connor called forth in people who saw her in her home at Andalusia in order to explain the complexity of her last stories, some of which, as I have already noted, are based on the apocalyptic theme of rising in order to converge. But none of the stories in this final volume have that fierce quality seen in a story like "A Good Man Is Hard to Find." These earlier stories invoke a sense of the overpowering quality that evil can have in

---

[19]Anna Balakian, *The Symbolist Movement* (New York: Random House, 1967) 51.

[20]Louise Hardeman Abbot, "Remembering Flannery O'Connor," *Southern Literary Journal* 2 (Spring 1970): 6.

[21]Ibid.

[22]Ibid., 13.

certain lives, and for those who prefer the early work of O'Connor to the later work, these are the stories of greatest visionary power, the works, that is, which suggest the abyss of evil that human beings can sink into.

Lewis P. Simpson concluded his book *The Brazen Face of History* with Henry James's vision of what Simpson called the "detached, and no doubt Satanic, visage of history looming above the American Capitol."[23] Deeply influenced by James, largely through her association with Allen Tate and Caroline Gordon, O'Connor knew that she could not repeat James's, or Faulkner's, involvement with history. Faulkner, Welty, Warren and other Southern writers had, as Simpson has put it, assimilated history to memory, but the last word of books like *Absalom, Absalom!* and *Losing Battles* is doom, that is, the end of a way of life. O'Connor, however, was not overwhelmed by that sense of doom which she had inherited from Southern writers, going all the way back to Poe. She believed that another Southern life was possible, the life of a post-civil-rights South that is beginning to appear in some of the stories in *Everything That Rises Must Converge*. And through her association with Tate and Gordon she knew, probably better than even Faulkner, Welty, or Warren, that the values of the pre-civil-rights South had long been dying. As Thomas Daniel Young has pointed out in his seminal book, *The Past in the Present*, the decline and death of the old Southern values had begun even before the Civil War. In his examination of Tate's *The Fathers* and Faulkner's *The Unvanquished*, for instance, Young showed how individual and social narcissism had been eroding the values of white Southern culture even before the Civil War. And yet, Young suggested, Faulkner revealed "how through the Civil War the established social order may be destroyed and, at the same time, suggests the means by which some of the values of a traditional society may be perpetuated."[24] O'Connor fully accepted the decline and death of several layers of Southern culture—Federalist, Cotton Kingdom, the New South before civil rights. She did not need to struggle fictionally with the historical details of decline and death. She took up with the "doom" that the Tates, Faulkner, Welty, and Warren all present in their deepest work, and she dramatizes the diabolical aspects of this "doom." For her, as for Tate or Faulkner, this "doom" is centered in narcissism, the worship of a false

---

[23]Simpson, *Brazen Face of History*, 276.
[24]Thomas Daniel Young, *The Past in the Present* (Baton Rouge: Louisiana State University Press, 1982) 25.

self, created within the head by denying the heart. Yet in her vision of the apocalyptic revival of a post-civil-rights South, she showed how certain traditional values contained in religion, education, and government can help to form new communities that take into account a true human self growing from love and a common concern for all individuals.

Three stories in *Everything That Rises Must Converge* contain the old O'Connor literary magic in presenting the triumph of the diabolic in the lives of people who seek to live entirely from the old beliefs of a dying social order. Two other stories at the end of the volume contain limited apocalyptic insights that are more earthbound than her cosmic visions in "Revelation" and "The Lame Shall Enter First." In "Greenleaf," possibly the most successful of the three, O'Connor placed one of her powerful women at the center of a new-style, post-World War II plantation. The woman has one concern only—to rule "with an iron hand." The declining values of Old South plantation living mean nothing to her; succeeding as a successful modern farmer means everything. But without realizing it, she is at the end of her tether. For all her successful efforts, the protagonist is destroyed by a series of events that can only be called diabolical in the way O'Connor used the term. For the author the diabolical manifested itself as a force leading to psychic and sometimes physical disintegration. In her story "The Comforts of Home," a young man falls under the spell of the old house he inhabits with his mother. Unable to move creatively into the future, he succumbs to voices of the past that inhabit the house. He loses contact with the present and, trying to live from the remembered past of his father's power, he falls into a meaningless violence. In another story, "A View of the Woods," the protagonist puts the past firmly behind him and opts totally for a future of "progress" in the New South. Mr. Fortune sells off his land in name of "progress": "[H]e would never have been able to sell off any lots of it had it not been for progress" (*CS*, 337). His vision of progress is quite clear to him:

> He wanted to see a paved highway in front of his house with plenty of new-model cars on it, he wanted to see a supermarket store across the road from him, he wanted to see a gas station, a motel, a drive-in-picture-show within easy distance. Progress had suddenly set all this in motion (*CS*, 337).

Yet Mr. Fortune, like all of O'Connor's strong-minded protagonists, is destroyed by his very attempts to make his dream of progress come true. He is killed in one of those mysterious ways set in motion by the diabolical powers that so often operate in O'Connor's stories. His own nine-year-old granddaughter, whom he has selected to be his heir, is driven into a mad rage by Mr. Fortune's obsession, a rage that leads to his death.

In O'Connor's stories diabolical powers are usually activated by the will to power of an individual who has succumbed to a rigid mind-set. The powers of an obsessed individual, in certain mysterious ways, bring ruin not only to the individual but to some of those with whom he or she is associated. O'Connor's continued use of this theme doubtless is connected with her awareness of those powerful men and women in the Southern past who believed they could create a new nation based on cotton-producing plantations. Yet in her own world of the mid-twentieth century she found this same Southern will to power at work in many areas of life, based as it was so often on what Jacques Derrida continually refers to in his prolific work as logocentricity—a mind-centeredness directed toward a logos system that denies inherent differences existing in human affairs. O'Connor would, had she lived longer, undoubtedly not have become a deconstructionist; she was too much of a religious rationalist to do that. As I have noted in an article on the relationship of her thought and work to both New Criticism and Deconstruction, there are nevertheless aspects of her fiction that can be studied in terms of deconstruction.[25] In a speech he made at Georgia State University in 1984, I heard Derrida succinctly define deconstruction as "decomposition." In much of her fiction, O'Connor wrote about the decomposing of both individuals and of organizations like farms, families, and businesses. Yet O'Connor was sometimes at her best in revealing the possibility of new life beyond decomposition. To sum up the chief difference between the process of deconstructing and that of reconstructing in O'Connor, the former is accompanied by destructive forces connected with self-centeredness and lovelessness whereas the latter contains within it some awareness of love and of a unifying connection between the essential humanity of one individual and another.

In her two concluding stories in *Everything That Rises Must Converge*, O'Connor reveals the possibilities of reconciliation between two groups whose struggles with each other she was well acquainted— men and women everywhere and blacks and whites in the rural South. It was

---

[25]Ted R. Spivey, "Flannery O'Connor, the New Criticism, and Deconstruction," *Southern Review* 23/2 (April 1987): 271-81.

as if, in "Parker's Back" and "Judgement Day," she believed she could make significant fictional statements about three psychic traumas of modern times—sexism, racism, and religious bigotry. In "Parker's Back" she writes of a woman who is obsessed with her particular abstract ideas about religion. Her religious bigotry makes her at first adopt an attitude of superiority to a young man who courts her. Later when the suitor seeks to please her with what she considers to be an unorthodox expression of religion, her ingrained bigotry drives her to reject his love. Yet hope is held out for both people because, in spite of her rejection, the young man continues to love the woman. In "Judgement Day," an even more difficult problem is partially overcome by the end of the story. The racism of a yeoman farmer who deserts the care of his daughter in New York to go home to join his friends is at last overcome when the man realizes that he indeed loves the black friend his racist ideas had for years made him look down on. O'Connor in both stories suggests the possibility of renewal through personal rediscovery and with that rediscovery the finding of an essential unity that exists between all people.

In both stories she turns not to religious vision, as she does in "Revelation," for a solution to the kind of abstract thinking that can lead to lovelessness and diabolism, but instead she uses aspects of existence she herself might have called "romantic." The young man in "Parker's Back" is sometimes motivated by what O'Connor in her first novel called "wise blood," as when "once in a rapture, Parker had obeyed whatever instinct of this kind had come to him" (*CS*, 527). And in "Judgement Day," Tanner in his dreams sees his true homecoming with his black friend Coleman and realizes, even as he is dying, that love is possible beyond the abstract hatreds spawned by racism. Thus I would reiterate that O'Connor's vision of the human "rise" toward generalized feelings of unity suggests an inevitable tug in her work toward the kind of cosmic visions she found in the work of Teilhard and others. Finally, I might mention one other writer who was too young to influence O'Connor but whose own attitudes are sometimes similar to hers. That writer is Alice Walker.

One of the ironies of Southern literature is that Alice Walker once lived within walking distance of the O'Connor dairy farm, Andalusia. Walker admits to a great admiration for O'Connor's work and has said that they both were influenced by many of the same social and religious forces. In this connection Walker has said, "In the South, everyone has to deal with the fact that there is a radical Christianity." Walker has sought both in her fiction and in essays like those in *Living by the Word*, most of which were written after the publication of *The Color Purple*, the solution to problems like racism and sexism. Like O'Connor, she believes that these failures "to rise and converge" must be overcome through a search for the basic harmony existing both in the universe and in the individual.

O'Connor had sometimes consciously sought to reject the kind of cosmic approach Walker takes as being "romantic." To Hawkes she had written that she did not belong to the "romantic tradition," and to me she had said and written that she could not accept my own "romantic" view of the spirit (*HB*, 456). But her continuing interest in and use of the ideas of Teilhard suggest indeed that she had a romantic side that she never came fully to grips with. The fact that, though desperately ill, she was still working on "Parker's Back" less than two weeks before she died reveals that continuing interest in the romantic (that is, the intuitive, instinctive, indefinable) which she reveals in the character of Enoch Emery in *Wise Blood*, a character she consciously saw as part of herself. By June 1959, I saw changes in her attitudes toward Zen Buddhism and even hope for changes in her attitude toward Protestantism. In writing of a book she was reviewing on Zen and Japanese culture, she stated: "I took it up as a burden but I find it very interesting and it's easy to see what attracts the beat people" (*CS*, 337). I had originally discussed Zen with her in connection with the new Beat writers of the late fifties and had urged her to explore this new literary and religious trend.

One of the great questions that must inevitably be raised about O'Connor is how far she would have gone on developing her "romantic" viewpoints. How "cosmic" in the Alice Walker sense would she have become? In the letter quoted above, she makes it clear in considering the movement of Beat literature that she would never let go of the concept of a discipline firmly based in what for her was the preeminent religious expression of the Catholic Church. Yet she does concede that the Beat position has a critique of society she can agree with:

> Certainly some revolt against our exaggerated materialism is long overdue. They [the Beats] seem to know a good many of the right things to run away from, but to lack any necessary discipline. They call themselves holy but holiness costs and so far as I can see they pay nothing (*CS*, 337).

One of the great O'Connor themes at the end of her life was the need for a social renewal beyond the obsessive materialistic kind of Cartesian control she so often satirized. But better than most she knew that vision had to be linked with a "necessary discipline." Teilhard gave her the great metaphor of the rising and merging of peoples into creative social life. There is no answer to the question of how much more she would have developed the metaphor of rising in order to converge that is found in her last creative work. Yet it is still necessary to pose this question: where was Flannery O'Connor headed?

Where, as a Literary Artist, Was O'Connor Headed?

As one who knew O'Connor well and as one who has studied and taught her work for nearly forty years, I can say that I have no final statement about the direction her work would have taken had she lived. Yet I can speak about the direction in which her life seemed to be moving, at least, that is, her professional life. She spoke to me several times and wrote in letters to me about the role of woman of letters that she was beginning to assume at the end of her life. We may be sure, if she had lived longer, that she would, like her mentor Caroline Gordon, have become herself a mentor to at least a few other men and women seeking to write well about the South. And by now she probably would have been awarded the Nobel Prize; at least her present literary reputation throughout the world indicates just that.

Although her literary outlook was both national and international, O'Connor was, as a person and a writer, very much a Southerner. In fact, in asking me to write critically about her work and in reading and commenting on two articles I wrote about her, she gave every indication that she wanted to help bring into existence a school of criticism that could grapple in new ways with a Southern literature that had by 1960 become truly post-Faulknerian. She always paid homage to Faulkner, but she grasped so deeply his greatness as a writer that she knew that Southern writing after 1960 would have to move in new directions. She had less personal vanity than any artist I have ever met, but she knew her own work was a beacon pointing toward literary visions of a South after Faulkner, after the civil rights struggle, and after the completion of the urbanization of the South. Even if her own creative writing had diminished, she would have made a great contribution to her region and to her nation as a woman of letters writing essays, giving lectures and personal encouragement to other writers, and rethinking both the literary and social problems of the region.

Yet one may well ask if her creative writing would have declined or stopped altogether. Was it possible that, as she completed the stories contained in *Everything That Rises Must Converge*, she was going through a period of depression of the sort known to many artists? And would this period have been only a prelude to a new creative outburst? A figure she resembles in many ways—T. S. Eliot—went through just such a period in the early thirties before finding the energy to write the *Quartets* and his major dramas. In her prescient introduction to the O'Connor letters, Sally Fitzgerald ended by quoting from the author's letter to Sr. Mariella Gable: "I've been writing eighteen years and I've reached the point where I can't do again what I can do well and the larger things I need to do now, I doubt my capacity for doing" (*HB*, xix). I have in earlier chapters spoken of the growing pessimism in O'Connor's letters and conversations concerning the reception of her work and her lectures at colleges. The publication in 1960 of *The Violent Bear It Away* marked a turning away from her work by some critics who had praised her earlier writing. O'Connor never repeated herself and this novel was something new, containing as it did a vision no one I knew could really comprehend at the time of its publication. I fault myself still for the uncomprehending letter I wrote her upon receiving and immediately reading the copy she sent me. I realized at the time that I could not respond creatively to this novel; I can now only just begin to grasp it, both existentially and intellectually. As for her lectures, the reception of them sometimes became acrimonious when listeners or participants in seminars realized she was treading literary and religious depths beyond what they could accept.

Those who have written of O'Connor as a recluse and always as a seriously ill person physically have had no trouble linking her depression to her physical condition. But Fitzgerald in *The Habit of Being* made it clear that not until late in her life did her illness become deeply serious. She wrote that "A new and somewhat ominous note" was sounded in a letter of 13 December 1963 concerning "a possibly serious development in Flannery's fragile health" (*HB*, 554). Near Christmas 1963, treatment for anemia occurred, and, as Fitzgerald stated, "she began to work intensely . . . on the stories with which she hoped to round out the collection planned for the fall" (*HB*, 559). The anemia, she learned in February 1964, was caused by a benign tumor. An operation on the tumor reactivated Flannery's lupus, and from then until her death in August of the same year her health steadily declined.

In the summer of 1963, O'Connor seemed to have put behind her for a time both her lupus and her depression at any opposition to her writing and her earlier lecturing, though, of course, she was never well in the ordinary sense of that word. But she did complete a chapter of a new novel to be called "Why Do the Heathen Rage?" that appeared in *Esquire*. Publication in this popular magazine even brought her the kind of local acceptance she might once have wanted. On 22 June 1963, she wrote "A": "I am much amused by the local reaction to my appearing in *Esquire* . . . you would think that at last I was really going places. I didn't know so many people took the thing" (*HB*, 526). The letter contains the kind of happy literary remarks found in earlier letters of a happier period. She had read a piece on one of her favorite philosophers, Hannah Arendt: "Cal [Robert Lowell] writes a good letter in her defense," she noted (*HB*, 526). She mentioned an article by Norman Mailer in the copy of *Esquire* that she planned to read. Mailer and his fellow New York writers irked O'Connor for more than one reason, but her comment on this group is amusingly condescending: "I gather he is attacking a lot of selected writers but I haven't read it. These literary young men spend a great deal of time dissecting each others failures . . . " (*HB*, 526). The fact that she was in good spirits can be seen in the kind of stern rebuke she could succinctly deliver to friends like "A," Bill Sessions, or myself; witness this rebuke to "A": "Your views on morality are for never-never land. We don't live in it" (*HB*, 526). But the letters of 1964 reveal a growing awareness of her real condition. Lupus often brings with it sudden seizures of anger, but there still remained her indomitable courage, the desire to finish work on her second and last volume of stories.

Several stories in *Everything That Rises Must Converge* indicate that she was attempting to create characters with sufficient psychological depth and complexity to speak personally to her growing number of sophisticated readers. She had known for some years that she was, incorrectly, of course, being grouped with writers like Erskine Caldwell and Carson McCullers who were known primarily for their grotesque characters. Writing to Cecil Dawkins in November 1963, she suggested the possibility of a dramatization of *Wise Blood*, but concluded: "If the times were different I would suggest that [a dramatization], but I think it would just be taken for the super-grotesque sub-Carson McCullers sort of thing that I couldn't stand the sight or sound of" (*HB*, 546). In stories like "The Enduring Chill," "Parker's Back," and "Revelation," as well as in the fragment of a novel published in *Esquire*, she was searching for new psychological depths to match the vision of renewed spiritual life she was continuing to discover for herself in Teilhard's work. Lewis P. Simpson has said that O'Connor's "stories follow a compelling aesthetic of revelation," even while noting, at the same time, that her stories "employ a series of characters who lack the subtleties of the self as a creature of modern secular history."[1] From *Wise Blood* on there was the "aesthetic of revelation" in O'Connor's work, but little complexity of character until we encounter Rayber in *The Violent Bear It Away*. But from this novel to her fragment "Why Do the Heathen Rage?" there is a conscious fictional quest for psychological complexity.

What I believed she needed in her work was an even deeper plunge than she had already taken into the kind of Blakean vision that Caroline Gordon had early discovered in her work. I suggested several times to her a consideration of the kind of psychic dreams that had been explored in depth by C. G. Jung, the famous psychologist that she had been seriously reading (as well as reading about) before I met her. I never thought she should become a Jungian, or, for that matter, a follower of any psychological school. But a consideration of Jung's life and work, particularly as we find it presented in his *Memories, Dreams, Reflections*, might have led her to consider certain possibilities concerning solutions to problems presented by the unconscious mind in our time. In the last letter she wrote me, on 17 March 1964, after my wife and I had to postpone several trips to see her, she seemed to reject my own discussion of the possibilities of the effect of certain types of dreams on literary work: "[L]et me tell you again that I have no interest whatsoever in all the dream business. . . . Into that I can't go with you and there's an end to it" (*HB*, 570). In earlier years she had in several conversations with me expressed an interest in the relationship between dreams and the creative process, and I can account for her harshness in this last letter primarily in terms of sudden bursts of anger, due in large part to a lupus newly reactivated in early 1964, that she would sometimes vent on close friends.

I did not myself understand what direction my own discussions with her about dream and creativity were taking until sometime after her death. In fact, I was greatly enlightened after a discussion I had with Joseph K. Davis, an authority on Southern literature who has for more than thirty years read, taught, and written about her work. A Jungian

---

[1]Lewis P. Simpson, *The Brazen Face of History* (Baton Rouge: Louisiana State University Press, 1980) 248.

himself, Davis pointed out to me that the basic problem concerning the visionary aspect of O'Connor's work was her failure to fully encounter the creative aspects of her own anima archetype, that is, of the power of the feminine contained in the psyche. Elizabeth Drew in her Jungian study of T. S. Eliot noted how in a poem like "Marina" a positive anima image accompanies the healing forces working within the psyche of the poet, forces which overcome the power of negative shadow images. I myself in my Jungian studies of the psychic healing of Conrad Aiken and Walker Percy noted this type of appearance of positive anima images in literary visions which record an inner healing.[2] The need for more images of creativity and hope, both anima and mandala images, can be seen in most of O'Connor's profoundest work, where shadow imagery dominates all other imagery. For Jung the shadow, or destructive side of life, is represented for many Christians in terms of images of Satan. I understand, even as I write this, that O'Connor would have spoken against a kind of Catholic unorthodoxy that is no doubt contained in what I am writing, but for me her own sense of orthodoxy was based far too much on too literal an interpretation of scripture and of theology. Possibly some of this theological rigidity is indeed contained in her final letter to me. And yet that side of her which I earlier called the "outsider" was always reaching beyond rigidity to new vision.

I have already pointed out aspects of the Devil in her work which to some readers are downright frightening. I can only point out in rebuttal to her own prevailing sense of evil that in the practice of the world's higher religions—as we know that practice in historical terms—the image of the Devil has, for the most part, not been at the center of the religious quest. Certain cults—like that of the late twentieth-century revival of Islam in Iran—often make the shadow archetype their dominant image, but the images of psychic renewal are overwhelmingly central to the ritual and symbology of the world's religions. Davis, in his masterly study comparing and contrasting Faulkner and O'Connor, went to the very heart of this matter in considering her fiction: "Her formulations [of the

---

[2]Ted R. Spivey, *The Writer as Shaman: The Pilgrimages of Conrad Aiken and Walker Percy* (Macon GA: Mercer University Press, 1986). See also Edward Butscher's *Conrad Aiken: Poet of the White Horse Vale* (Athens: University of Georgia Press, 1988) 456: "Ted R. Spivey had been virtually alone among Aiken critics in appreciating the Jungian nature of the solution supplied by 'Changing Mind' to the problem of locating a transcendental aesthetic in a modern skeptical context."

Devil], if often quite beautiful in their artistic executions, are terrifying and ugly in their revelations of the awful powers of the demonic in human life."[3] Davis also related the concern of O'Connor's violence and demonic forces to the Southern sense of defeat and historical humiliation: "Uniquely American, if in a paradoxical way, the Southern writer understands from his heart the meaning of defeat, grief, and pain in a ruined, shattered present."[4] Yet even as we face the sense of gloom in O'Connor, we must be aware that there are also images of renewal in her work, beginning with *Wise Blood*. Enoch Emery, the child with "wise blood," is one image, but as a character he ends lost and bewildered because his innocence goes at last unrecognized and unaccepted. In Teilhard's formula of rising and converging, O'Connor sought images of renewal, but Teilhard's limitations I have already noted. Yet, had she lived longer, O'Connor, with new visions of transcendence supplied by her reading of Teilhard and others, may well have written a major work suggesting the possibilities of new life, that necessary renewal of creative energy if the kind of loss and sense of failure Davis finds in the South is to be at last overcome.

I struck a chord with O'Connor when I gave her a copy of Martin Buber's *The Eclipse of God*. I think it was because Buber's work contains a vision pointing beyond the great modernist belief in the "death of God" and the sense of nihilism that sometimes accompanies that belief. I only wish I had given her books by another religious existentialist who, like Buber, saw beyond a modernism almost overpowered by visions of ruin and dehumanization: this was Nicolas Berdyaev, the Russian inspired by the religious visions of Dostoevski. Berdyaev had a sense of apocalyptic renewal that in his later work seems stronger than the vision of apocalyptic destruction. After all death and renewal are central to all authentic apocalyptic vision. In one of his last works, *Truth and Revelation*, Berdyaev wrote of the revelation of renewal that is possible for everyone, even children: "[T]here have always been men and women in whom there was fire which has not cooled down."[5] O'Connor was such a person, and

---

[3]Joseph K. Davis, "Time and the Demonic in William Faulkner and Flannery O'Connor," *Studies in the Literary Imagination* 20/2 (Fall 1987): 143.

[4]Ibid.

[5]Nicolas Berdyaev, *Truth and Revelation*, trans. R. McFrench (New York: Collier Books, 1962) 148.

I think that increasingly her similarities to her greatest fictional master, James Joyce, will be studied.

Both Joyce and O'Connor knew the violence that can be generated by certain types of religious zealotry, and both wrote of individuals who, in plunging into the modern city to escape their religious past, could never totally let go of their inherited vision and sought to reach back to psychic roots in efforts to find a hope and belief that would bring with it the release of long-suppressed creative powers. Both wrote of the beauties of a nature they loved and of a past they honored, but both willingly followed the modern quester into the most secular of cities, a quester seeking another and a better city beyond the urban sprawl of the late twentieth century.

O'Connor did not live long enough to write of the new city that would appear, though in her last great story, "Revelation," she does give us her own vision of what St. Augustine called "the pilgrim City of God," a city moving into a new age of concord. Of this new age and new city Joyce would write in *Finnegans Wake* of the City of Is, as he called it, proclaiming "Atlanst," or "Atlanta, at Last," as he first wrote it. Thus Joyce in his last book transformed the decaying modern city of Dublin into a new heavenly city. Strangely enough, Joyce in the second paragraph of *Finnegans Wake* writes of "the stream Oconee exaggerated themselves to Laurens County's gorgios," referring to the Oconee River which runs past Milledgeville, south for twenty miles to Toomsboro and then a few more miles to Laurens county and Dublin, Georgia. Thus Joyce, by referring to the two Dublins in Europe and America and by using a Creek Indian name for a river, Oconee, which is also the Gaelic word for alas, announces his theme of the struggle of fathers and sons, mothers and daughters, a necessary struggle in the most significant mythic theme of the *Wake*: life, death, rebirth.[6]

Generational struggle is a quintessential O'Connor theme, and through it her quester is projected forth from his deeply felt but dying Southern culture to find new values in a new kind of city that O'Connor and Joyce of the *Wake* both suggest may yet appear in the future. The miracle of the Joyce vision in the *Wake* is that from family struggle, from pain, and from the dying old city must spring the city of new, beautiful men and women. For O'Connor, the new age begins with the violent

---

[6]James Joyce, *Finnegans Wake* (New York: Viking Press, 1958).

seizure of the Kingdom of God which awaits the new quester turned prophet. Somehow an Irishman of Europe had reached across an ocean to touch a younger Irish-American woman in ways beyond any student's understanding of this relationship. Possibly they both held to a vision based in their Irish past. Certainly there is no modern intertextual relationship any stronger than that which envelopes Joyce and O'Connor.

Joyce and O'Connor speak in their last works of a death of one cultural order that makes way for another. The sprawling city without order or direction is part of the necessary journey to this new order. The O'Connor ordeal, like the Joyce ordeal, was to love the old order and to accept with a long alas its slow dying, to embrace cities they loved and hated, fully accepted and fully rejected. For O'Connor the prophecy of a new age of the triumph of the megalopolitan sprawl over all rural and urban forms of culture is fulfilled at the home where she did most of her writing, that is, Andalusia, the dairy farm where her mother Regina supported in comfort the two of them. Today, across the road from Andalusia stands a Holiday Inn. By 1988 part of Andalusia was becoming a suburb of Milledgeville with an O'Connor Drive already laid out for a subdivision on land that once nourished Regina's dairy cows. Statisticians forecast a time when Atlanta will stretch north to Chattanooga, south to Macon and Milledgeville. In fact, Highway 441 from the old town of Milledgeville to Lake Sinclair had by 1988 become one of the depersonalized "strips" that surround both towns and cities in America. I remember first hearing the term "motel culture" from O'Connor's lips in 1959. She had found a vision of it in Vladimir Nabokov's *Lolita*. She spoke the words with a strange fascination and, I am sure, without either of us quite knowing it, with a prophetic understanding.

Even as O'Connor's world is turning into the new, formless cities of the end of the century, other writers hear in her work the sounds of new life. Thus Alice Walker can write in her essay "Beyond the Peacock: The Reconstruction of Flannery O'Connor": "She was for me the first great modern writer from the South."[7] For Walker, "classic O'Connor" is the moment of supreme revelation when the individual faces his or her own limitations and "comprehends 'the true frontiers of her own inner country.' "[8] For Walker, and writers younger still of all races and classes and

---

[7]Alice Walker, "Beyond the Peacock: The Reconstruction of Flannery O'Connor," in *Critical Essays on Flannery O'Connor*, ed. Friedman and Clark, 76.
[8]Ibid., 74.

both genders, O'Connor may well point to revelations of a time beyond the painful changes of a strange century. It well may be that, as Walker stated, "*essential* O'Connor is not about race at all, which is why it is so refreshing, coming as it does, out of such a *racial* culture."[9] It is, as Walker rightly pointed out, about prophets and prophecy, about revelation and grace. All those who continue reading Flannery O'Connor's writing may well remain dismayed by her early death, but they will always be thankful for the revelation she gave her nation concerning its past, present, and future.

---

[9]Ibid., 77.

Selected Bibliography

Abbot, Louise Hardeman. "Remembering Flannery O'Connor." *Southern Literary Journal* 2 (Spring 1970): 3-25.

Asals, Frederick. *Flannery O'Connor: The Imagination of Extremity.* Athens: University of Georgia Press, 1982.

Balakian, Anna. *The Symbolist Movement.* New York: Random House, 1967.

Berdyaev, Nicolas. *Truth and Revelation.* Translated by R. McFrench. New York: Collier Books, 1962.

Bloom, Harold, editor. *Flannery O'Connor.* New York: Chelsea House, 1986.

Burgess, Anthony. *The Novel Now.* New York: Pegasus, 1967.

Butscher, Edward. *Conrad Aiken: Poet of the White Horse Vale.* Athens: University of Georgia Press, 1988.

Campbell, Joseph. *Myths to Live By.* New York: Viking Press, 1972.

Carr, Virginia Spencer. *The Lonely Hunter: A Biography of Carson McCullers.* New York: Carroll and Graf Publishers, 1985.

Christiani, Leon. *Evidence of Satan in the Modern World.* New York: Aaron Books, 1980.

Coles, Robert. *Flannery O'Connor's South.* Baton Rouge: Louisiana State University, 1980.

Davis, Joseph K. "Time and the Demonic in William Faulkner and Flannery O'Connor." *Studies in the Literary Imagination* 20/2 (Fall 1987): 123-43.

Drake, Robert. *Flannery O'Connor: A Critical Essay.* Grand Rapids MI: William B. Eerdmans, 1966.

Finley, James. *Merton's Palace of Nowhere: A Search for God through Awareness of the True Self.* Notre Dame: Ave Maria Press, 1983.

Fitzgerald, Sally. "The Andalusian Sibyl." *Southern Living* (May 1983): 65.

Forster, E. M. *Aspects of the Novel.* New York: Harcourt, Brace & World, 1954.

Fox-Genovese, Elizabeth. *Within the Plantation Household: Black and White Women of the Old South.* Chapel Hill: University of North

Carolina Press, 1988.

Friedman, Marvin L. and Lewis A. Lawson, editors. *The Added Dimension: The Mind and Art of Flannery O'Connor*. New York: Fordham University Press, 1966.

Gardner, John. *On Becoming a Novelist*. New York: Harper & Row, 1983.

Gilman, Richard. "A Life of Letters." *New York Times Book Review* (18 March 1979): 32.

Gilman, Richard. "On Flannery O'Connor." *Conversations with Flannery O'Connor*, edited by Rosemary M. Magee. Jackson: University of Mississippi Press, 1987.

Hawkes, John. "Flannery O'Connor's Devil." *Sewanee Review* 70/3 (Summer 1962): 395-407.

Hicks, Granville. "A Writer at Home with Her Heritage." *Saturday Review* (12 May 1962): 22-23.

Hyman, Stanley Edgar. *Flannery O'Connor*. Minneapolis: University of Minnesota Press, 1966.

Johnson, Paul. *A History of Christianity*. New York: Atheneum, 1987.

Joyce, James. *Finnegans Wake*. New York: Viking Press, 1958.

Kaufmann, Walter. *Existentialism from Dostoevsky to Sartre*. New York: Meridian Books, 1956.

Kessler, Edward. *Flannery O'Connor and the Language of Apocalypse*. Princeton: Princeton University Press, 1986.

Kinney, Arthur F. *Flannery O'Connor's Library: Resources of Being*. Athens: University of Georgia Press, 1985.

Magee, Rosemary M., editor. *Conversations with Flannery O'Connor*. Jackson: University of Mississippi Press, 1987.

Martin, Carter. *The True Country: Themes in the Fiction of Flannery O'Connor*. Nashville: Vanderbilt University Press, 1969.

Martin, Malachi. *Jesus Now*. New York: Popular Library, 1973.

May, John R. *The Pruning Word: The Parables of Flannery O'Connor*. Notre Dame: University of Notre Dame Press, 1976.

Montgomery, Marion. *Why Flannery O'Connor Stayed at Home*. Volume 1 of *The Prophetic Poet and the Spirit of the Age*. La Salle IL: Sherwood, Sugden and Co., 1981.

Moore, Harry T. *Twentieth-Century French Literature*. New York: Dell Publishing Co., 1966.

Nichols, Loxley F. "Flannery O'Connor's 'Intellectual Vaudeville': Masks of Mother and Daughter." *Studies in Literary Imagination* 20/2

(Fall 1987): 15-30.

O'Connor, Flannery. *The Complete Short Stories of Flannery O'Connor.* Introduced by Robert Giroux. New York: Farrar, Straus, and Giroux, 1986.

——. *Everything That Rises Must Converge.* Introduced by Robert Fitzgerald. New York: Farrar, Straus, and Giroux, 1965.

——. *The Habit of Being: Letters of Flannery O'Connor.* Edited by Sally Fitzgerald. New York: Farrar, Straus, and Giroux, 1979.

——. *Mystery and Manners: Occasional Prose.* Edited by Sally and Robert Fitzgerald. New York: Farrar, Straus, and Giroux, 1969.

——. *The Violent Bear It Away.* New York: Farrar, Straus, and Cudahy, 1960.

——. *Wise Blood.* New York: Noonday Press, 1962.

Oates, Joyce Carol. "The Visionary Art of Flannery O'Connor," in *Flannery O'Connor*, edited by Harold Bloom. New York: Chelsea House, 1986.

Olson, Steven. "Tarwater's Hats." *Studies in the Literary Imagination.* 20/2 (Fall 1987): 37-49.

Paulson, Suzanne M. *Flannery O'Connor: A Study of the Short Fiction.* Boston: Twayne Publishers, 1988.

Percy, Walker. *The Message in the Bottle: How Queer Man Is, How Queer Language Is, and What One Has to Do with the Other.* New York: Farrar, Straus, and Giroux, 1979.

Picard, Max. *The Flight from God.* Translated by Marianne Kuschnitzky and J. M. Cameron. Introduced by Gabriel Marcel. Chicago: Henry Regnery Co., 1951.

Rubin, Louis D., Jr. "Flannery O'Connor and the Bible Belt" in *The Added Dimension: The Mind and Art of Flannery O'Connor*, edited by Melvin J. Friedman and Lewis A. Lawson, 49-72. New York: Fordham University Press, 1966.

Sessions, William A. "A Correspondence," in *The Added Dimension: The Mind and Art of Flannery O'Connor*, edited by Melvin J. Friedman and Lewis A. Lawson, 209-25. New York: Fordham University Press, 1966.

Simpson, Lewis P. *The Brazen Face of History: Studies in the Literary Consciousness in America.* Baton Rouge: Louisiana State University Press, 1980.

Smith, Page. *The Shaping of America.* 3 Volumes. New York: McGraw-Hill Book Co., 1980.

Spivey, Ted R. "Flannery O'Connor, James Joyce and the City." *Studies in the Literary Imagination* 20/2 (Fall 1987): 87-96.

——. "Flannery O'Connor: Georgia's Theological Storyteller" in *The Humanities in the Contemporary South*, 1-17. School of Arts and Sciences Research Papers number 17. Atlanta: Georgia State College, 1968.

——. "Flannery's South: Don Quixote Rides Again." *Flannery O'Connor Bulletin* 1 (Fall 1972): 46-53.

——. "Flannery O'Connor's View of God and Man." *Studies in Short Fiction* I (Spring 1964): 200-206.

——. "Flannery O'Connor's Quest for a Critic." *Flannery O'Connor Bulletin* 15 (1987): 29-34.

——. "Flannery O'Connor, the New Criticism, and Deconstruction." *Southern Review* 23/2 (April 1987): 271-81.

——. *The Writer as Shaman: The Pilgrimages of Conrad Aiken and Walker Percy*. Macon: Mercer University Press, 1986.

Tate, Mary Barbara. "Flannery O'Connor at Home in Milledgeville." *Studies in the Literary Imagination* 20/2 (Fall 1987): 31-36.

Taylor, Jerome. *In Search of Self*. Cambridge MA: Cowley Publications, 1986.

Waldron, Ann. *Close Connections: Caroline Gordon and the Southern Renaissance*. New York: G. P. Putnam's Sons, 1987.

Walker, Alice. "Beyond the Peacock: The Reconstruction of Flannery O'Connor." in *Critical Essays on Flannery O'Connor* edited by Melvin J. Friedman and Beverly Lyon Clark, 71-81. Boston: G. K. Hall and Son, 1985.

Wehr, Gerhard. *Jung: A Biography*. Translated by David M. Weeks. Boston: Shambaba, 1987.

Young, Thomas Daniel. "Flannery O'Connor's View of the South: God's Earth and His Universe" *Studies in the Literary Imagination* 20/2 (Fall 1987): 5-14.

Young, Thomas Daniel. *The Past in the Present*. Baton Rouge: Louisiana State University Press, 1982.

Index

About the author

Ted R. Spivey is Regents' Professor of English Emeritus at Georgia State University. He received his A.B. degree from Emory University and his master's and doctorate degrees from the University of Minnesota. He has written six books of literary and philosophical criticism, including *The Writer as Shaman: The Pilgrimages of Conrad Aiken and Walker Percy*, (MERCER 1986) and has coauthored one study with Arthur Waterman. He lives in Atlanta, Georgia, with his wife Julia and has two children, Mary Leta and Andy.

Flannery O'Connor: The Woman, the Thinker, the Visionary.
by Ted R. Spivey.

Mercer University Press, Macon, Georgia 31210-3960.
ISBN 0-86554-467-0. Catalog and wh pick number MUP/H368.
Text and interior design, composition, and layout by Jon Parrish Peede.
Cover design by Stephen Hefner and Jon Parrish Peede.
Camera-ready pages composed on a Gateway 2000 via Wordperfect
    5.1/5.2 and printed on a LaserMaster 1000.
Text font: Times New Roman Postscript 11/10/9-point.
Printed and bound by Braun-Brumfield Inc., Ann Arbor MI 48106.